PENGUIN BOOKS

EVERYTHING YOU PRETEND TO KNOW
and Are Afraid Someone Will Ask

Lynette Padwa is a fifteen-year veteran of the publishing business and is currently at work on a book about mother-daughter relationships. Ms. Padwa lives in Los Angeles with her husband and son.

EVERYTHING YOU PRETEND TO KNOW

and Are Afraid Someone Will Ask

LYNETTE PADWA

PENGUIN BOOKS

PENGUIN BOOKS

Published by the Penguin Group

Penguin Books USA Inc., 375 Hudson Street, New York, New York 10014,
U.S.A.

Penguin Books Ltd, 27 Wrights Lane, London W8 5TZ, England

Penguin Books Australia Ltd, Ringwood, Victoria, Australia

Penguin Books Canada Ltd, 10 Alcorn Avenue, Toronto, Ontario, Canada
M4V 3B2

Penguin Books (N.Z.) Ltd, 182–190 Wairau Road, Auckland 10, New Zealand

Penguin Books Ltd, Registered Offices: Harmondsworth, Middlesex, England

First published in Penguin Books 1996

5   7   9   10   8   6

A NOTE TO THE READER

This book is intended only to inform readers on certain selected topics and is not
meant to substitute for professional advice applicable to specific situations. Neither the author nor the publisher can be held responsible for any consequence of
the use by anyone of the information contained herein.

LIBRARY OF CONGRESS CATALOGING IN PUBLICATION DATA
Padwa, Lynette.
Everything you pretend to know and are
afraid someone will ask/Lynette Padwa.
p.   cm.
Includes bibliographical references.
ISBN 0 14 05.1322 1 (pbk.)
1. Questions and answers.   2. Vocabulary.   I. Title.
AG195.P336   1995
031.02—dc20   95–15763

Printed in the United States of America
Set in Sabon
Designed by Claudyne Bedell

For Brett

✳

ACKNOWLEDGMENTS

✳

My appreciation to Peter Engel, Howard Cohl, and the people at Affinity Publishing for their support. A heartfelt thank-you to Lisa Gabbert, Dean Harris, and Lani Scheman for their invaluable and imaginative research. Finally, many thanks to my family and to my husband, Brett Palmer, for his sense of humor and his enthusiasm.

CONTENTS

✳

It's a typical lunch hour.

You're complaining about your boss's *laissez-faire* attitude while fretting over the cholesterol content of your sandwich —does avocado have good or bad cholesterol? Talk turns to the Fed's latest move (if interest rates go any higher, the economy's sure to take a dive!), but your mind wanders to last night's weather report. A low-pressure front is going to bring rain, and that's bad news because your car is in the shop. You've blown a head gasket, says your mechanic, and your air conditioner has a leak big enough to blast the ozone layer wide open. It's been a rough morning. Still, you bite the bullet and try not to wonder . . .

What does *laissez-faire* mean?
What is good and bad cholesterol?
What's "the Fed," and how does it control interest rates?
What's a low-pressure front? What kind of pressure are they talking about?
What's a gasket, and what makes it a "head" gasket? How can you "blow" one?

What does your air conditioner have to do with the ozone
  layer? What's ozone? Is it good or bad?
And finally—what does "bite the bullet" really *mean*?

If you spend your life feeling like you've walked in on the
second reel of the movie, relax. You *have* walked in on the
second reel—everyone has. Twentieth-century civilization has
fractured into countless areas of specialization. It would take
a genius with loads of spare time to stay abreast of all the
latest buzzwords, scientific breakthroughs, and cultural references. Even so, most people hate to ask, "What does that
mean?"—especially about terms like *interactive multimedia*
or *coup* or *acting out*, which everyone else tosses around with
knowing abandon.

Yet others, too, are skating on the thin ice of context, bluff-
ing their way through conversations. How do I know? Because when I enlisted the aid of friends and acquaintances
(educated, articulate citizens like you) to suggest questions for
this book, they confirmed it. An internationally published journalist wondered what made neofascism different from regular
old fascism. A psychologist wanted to know how fiber*optics*
can transmit sound. And everyone wanted to know the difference between a bear market and bull market.

Chuckling right now because you *do* know the difference
between bear and bull markets? Not so fast. What about
Bauhaus? Or the difference between a criminal suit and a civil
suit? What does electrical grounding do? None of these terms
is obscure; in fact, you've probably used them yourself without being quite sure what you were talking about. That was
the criteria for the questions included in this book: that they
increase your understanding of the events and words you en-
counter every day. True, I've included a few bits of information that aren't exactly essential to your survival, like the

difference between Cajun and Creole, or the strange practices of medieval grand juries. But I did it only if it was too fascinating to pass by.

As I pored through stacks of books and articles looking for answers to these queries, I began to understand why we're so often clueless about knowledge that's supposed to be "common." For one thing, all the new information we try to absorb each day tends to crowd out the old stuff, the basics we learned in high school. And even as we struggle to grasp the new facts, they are being distorted by news media or perverted by advertising campaigns. Aspirin, acetaminophen, ibuprofen, or naproxen—which is really the best cure for headaches? The experts can't keep it straight, so how can we?

But often the experts *can* keep it straight. Certain fields do evolve quickly, especially medicine and technology. Surprisingly, though, much of the information that's relevant to our daily lives stays consistent, even in those two fields. History, while always open to reinterpretation by scholars, is on basically solid ground too. The slippery stuff usually has to do with social sciences and psychology—the latter a field so new and fluid that its proponents themselves disagree as to whether it can legitimately be considered a hard science.

The answers here are by no means as thorough as those you'd find in books specializing on each particular topic. But they'll give you the facts you need to hold your head high at the lunch table, comprehend the evening news, and explain a thing or two to your twelve-year-old nephew—or at the very least, understand him when he explains things to you.

And by the way, ibuprofen and naproxen tie for the best headache relief, especially if they're chased with a cup of coffee. Happy browsing!

EVERYTHING YOU PRETEND TO KNOW
and Are Afraid Someone Will Ask

Deciphering Newsspeak

* * *

WHAT'S THE DIFFERENCE BETWEEN A CZAR, A MAGNATE, AND A MOGUL?
All three signify power, but czars, magnates, and moguls get
their power in different ways and lord it over different
realms. Czars tend to exist in the political world, moguls in
media and entertainment, and magnates in business.

Let's begin with *czar*. Usually a czar is a person who has
been appointed—not elected—to a particular office. When
President George Bush appointed William Bennett to head up
the "War on Drugs," Bennett was touted as the drug czar, a
title the Bush camp probably felt would lend him an aura of
absolute power. A look at news coverage over the past twenty
years yields an abundance of absolute rulers—energy czars,
baseball czars, AIDS czars, even strip-mining czars.

Czars in Russia did wield total power over their subjects.
The title was first used by Byzantine emperors, and in the
sixteenth century Ivan IV adapted it for his own use. By the
late 1700s the word *czar* had taken on some unattractive
attributes: Most Russians associated it with corruption and
oppression. Still, some romantic intellectuals longed for an
idealized czar, similar to a benevolent dictator, who would

serve his people wisely and have the power to put his noble plans swiftly into action. The Russian Revolution put an end to all that.

In the 1890s *czar* leaped over the Atlantic and into popular American culture as the nickname of House Speaker Thomas B. Reed, who was rather dictatorial in his use of parliamentary rules. The nickname was not intended as a compliment. Why, then, has czar become a good thing to be? It might have something to do with Americans' frustration at our government's inability to fix problems quickly. When people really want a problem solved, the president appoints someone to head up a program and calls him or her a czar—the implication being that this almighty ruler will plow through bureaucratic red tape. Interestingly, candidates don't run for office promising to be, for example, "Michigan's next czar." Americans will accept *appointed* czars because they can be fired. We'll flirt with the illusion of absolute power, but we're not too keen on the real thing.

Magnates don't wait to be appointed; they carve out their own realms of power. The term derives from the Latin *magnates,* and is roughly translated as "great person" or "nobleman." Today, magnate refers to a person who's been fantastically successful in business, crafting multimillion-dollar deals, building industries, determining the fate of thousands. Bill Gates, founder of Microsoft, is a magnate. He commands an astonishing amount of power over the way we conduct business because his company manufactures the operating systems used by most of the computers in this country. Who has more power, magnate Bill Gates or the appointed political czars? It's hard to say, since their realms are so different. But Gates will most likely hold on to his power much longer than his political counterparts will.

What about *moguls?* They inhabit the world of the media.

Mike Ovitz, head of Creative Artists Agency, and cable-TV whiz Ted Turner are media moguls. In essence, moguls are pretty interchangeable with magnates, and some media power brokers are referred to as moguls or magnates or both.

Mogul is a variation of the word *Mongol*. Moguls were Indian and Turkish emperors who held complete power over their subjects. In 1957 the *Times Literary Supplement* first used the word in connection with the film industry; it became the ideal way to suggest the utter control Hollywood's big chiefs had over their fiefdoms. Part czar (with the absolute power that implies), part magnate (dealing in the business world), the mogul somehow seems more ruthless, more sleazy, and more interesting than either.

WHAT IS SECULAR HUMANISM?

For the past decade, the term *secular humanism* has become a weapon. Conservatives call liberals secular humanists. Liberals respond by claiming that the term is too broad and vague to be defined meaningfully. In the mouths of conservatives and evangelicals, "secular humanist" has come to imply a person with an atheistic, perhaps even antireligious, philosophy and with dubious morals.

Strictly speaking, secular humanism is actually rather straightforward: *secular* means relating to worldly concerns; not overtly or specifically religious. *Humanism* is a philosophy that stresses the individual's worth, dignity, and as Webster's puts it, "capacity for self-realization through reason." Neither of these concepts would appear to bear the stamp of Satan.

The battle over the term rages on because of the type of deductive reasoning some conservatives apply to it: If a value system is based on the here-and-now reality of the world and the innate worth of humans—rather than on biblical text—

it may differ drastically from the traditional Judeo-Christian value system. It *may* differ, counter liberals, but it doesn't necessarily have to. Secular humanists may even share many of the same values as the most fundamentalist of Christians. Secular humanists have, however, come to these beliefs via the road of "reason, science, and democracy," according to Corliss Lamont in his book *The Philosophy of Humanism.*

Since the mid-1980s, when Senator Orrin Hatch of Utah revived the term (it had last been batted around in the early 1960s), the right has used secular humanism to lambaste any group, idea, law, or person whose agenda is perceived as too liberal. And because the definition of the term seems to depend on who's using it, countering these allegations is a little like punching balloons.

Why don't liberals stand up and proudly claim the label, as they have done with *feminism* and the infamous *card-carrying member of the ACLU*? Possibly because many who advocate such humanist values as tolerance and individual rights feel uncomfortable with the term's atheistic connotations. They believe in God and resent what they see as conservatives' attempts to co-opt the Almighty by labelling everyone with progressive ideas a secular humanist. For the record, a secular humanist does not automatically mean someone who is unpatriotic, heathen, anti-values, and anti-family. Just what it does mean seems to shift with the wind, which is why the term is such a powerful and dangerous one.

What's the difference between jail, prison, and the penitentiary?

There is a hierarchy to the language of criminal detention. Jails, which are used to detain people accused but not yet convicted of a crime, are the first step in the journey. Jails are for short-term detention, and they break down into sub-categories: *lockup* is jail in a police station; a *holding cell* is jail in a courthouse; and a *workhouse* is a county jail that houses a prisoner for eighteen months or less.

Hard-core prisoners end up in what used to be called *prison* or *the penitentiary*. Those terms were interchangeable, but both are passé now. Instead, these "places of confinement" are called *penal institutions* or the more up-to-date *correctional institutions*.

WHAT IS A SIGALERT?

SigAlert . . . Signal Alert? It makes sense, but it's wrong. The term *SigAlert* came about in honor of a Los Angeles radio broadcaster, Lloyd Sigmon, who was famous during the 1950s for breaking bulletins about traffic jams. In 1993 the term made its way into the Oxford English Dictionary, which defines it as "a message broadcast on the radio giving warning of traffic congestion; a traffic jam." A SigAlert, then, doesn't necessarily indicate an automobile accident. It just means the highways are backed up.

WHAT IS A SPIN DOCTOR?

Snake-oil salesman, smooth operator, confidence man . . . among this dubious group the spin doctor now holds a prominent place. A spin doctor is a person hired by a public figure to put a positive slant on that figure's actions and words. Needless to say, perhaps, spin doctors provide damage control; profound words and noble deeds don't require such creative interpretation. And spin doctors are certainly a response to the relentless media exposure public figures endure. The inane comments we all make now and then represent, for the famous, potential catastrophe. No wonder they like to travel with the defensive team close at hand.

It was just a decade ago that the term *spin doctor* made its way into the common vernacular. An editorial in the *New*

York Times on October 21, 1984, reported on the rather chilling scene that followed a televised Reagan–Mondale debate: "Tonight at about 9:30, seconds after the Reagan–Mondale debate ends, a bazaar will suddenly materialize in the press room. . . . A dozen men in good suits and women in silk dresses will circulate smoothly among the reporters, spouting confident opinions. They won't be just press agents trying to impart a favorable spin to a routine release. They'll be the Spin Doctors, senior advisers to the candidates."

Note the emphasis on the pedigree of the spin doctors. They are not mere PR flaks. Like the venerated play doctor whose magic touch turns a flop into a hit, the spin doctor is a professional at the top of his or her game. In the world of politics, spin doctors are often mentioned in the same breath as *handlers*. The handler supposedly instructs a politician (or celebrity) on how to behave; the spin doctor cleans up the mess if the instructions are flubbed or outright disobeyed. A spin doctor can also *be* a handler, creating a seamless control bubble around the queen bee.

Spin doctors are treated with derision by reporters (who, nevertheless, continue to give them airtime and print space) and by the general public. We want to believe that the famous, especially the people running the country, are smarter than we are, but the emergence of spin doctors makes it clear that not only won't these folks take responsibility for their actions, they're not even bright enough to think up their own excuses.

Will spin doctors be an inevitable part of the political scene from now on? It's hard to see why they wouldn't be. As one politician noted, "In this age, and in this country, public sentiment is everything. With it, nothing can fail; against it, nothing can succeed." That's what Abraham Lincoln thought in 1858, long before television. Spin doctors are probably here to stay.

WHAT IS CORPORATE DOWNSIZING?

At first this question might seem disingenuous: Everyone knows that *downsizing* is code for *firing*. It's true that downsizing means laying off large numbers of workers, usually permanently. What makes downsizing different is that in addition to being a corporate reaction to loss of profits, downsizing has evolved into a business philosophy that often guides personnel decisions even when a company is profitable.

There are many reasons for this. In the 1980s it became clear that American manufacturers needed to modernize their plants if they were going to compete effectively with Japan, West Germany, and other industrialized nations. They did modernize, to the point that they now can produce more items with fewer workers and sell them at prices that are competitive with the foreigners. The problem is that Americans aren't buying more goods, even at the lower prices, because the economy isn't strong enough. More people would need to find good jobs in order to buy more stuff. Who will hire them? Experts say most businesses would need to sell an additional 10 percent a year to justify hiring more workers, and few are doing that well. It's a vicious circle, and the result is that increased productivity doesn't necessarily mean profits for the manufacturer.

Where, then, can profits come from? Not from price increases—today's inflation-conscious public is unwilling to pay more each year for the same item. And there's always the pressure of underpriced foreign products crowding out the American-made ones. The only way for companies to maintain profits is by cutting the cost of labor. This begins when corporations decide they must "cut the fat." In the 1980s it meant modernizing plants and replacing workers with automated systems. In the 1990s the definition of "fat" has expanded to include white-collar workers, middle managers—every level of the workforce. All it takes is the development of the right computer program to render certain employees unnecessary. Because of this, downsizing does not cease just because a company has a good year. On the contrary, today's ideal manager is constantly looking for ways to decrease the workforce. A whole industry of corporate downsizing experts has evolved, complete with hired guns who'll set up shop to lay off workers so the permanent management won't have to hand out pink slips.

Downsizing tends to shift from industry to industry. One month it's banks, the next it's the aerospace industry, the next it's telecommunications. Even the service sector, where many of the "downsized" end up, is not immune to the trend. The reason: once again, modernization. Consider the bridal registry at your local department store. It used to be run by a kindly woman with a flair for home furnishings. Now you punch in a few names on a computer, and the printer spits out a list of desired items.

Downsizing may have begun as a euphemism for *firing*, but in the end, it might be the scarier of the two words. It's more relentless, as relentless as technology.

WHAT IS NEOFASCISM? IS IT DIFFERENT FROM FASCISM?

The dictionary's definition of *fascism* is straightforward enough: "A system of government characterized by rigid one-party dictatorship, forcible suppression of opposition, private economic enterprise under centralized government control, belligerent nationalism, racism, and militarism, etc." The people we generally think of as *neofascists*—skinhead soccer thugs and latter-day Aryan Nation geeks—are certainly racist and belligerent. Whether they've given much thought to "private economic enterprise under centralized government control" is another question. Today most violent ultra-right-wingers are called neofascists. Some gladly accept the term, some reject it.

Fascism began in Italy in the 1920s with Benito Mussolini, whose first group of fledgling fascists were mainly ex-anarchists, ex-socialists, and veterans who longed for order. Allegiance to a strong central authority was extremely appealing to them, and the charismatic Mussolini heeded the call. The key concept was authoritarianism: All opposition was crushed, and individual rights were swept away so that the state—and Mussolini—could rule with absolute power. Fervent nationalism was at the heart of the movement.

The word *fascist* quickly spread to other parts of Europe, where it was used when referring to any right-wing nationalist movement. It expanded to mean practically any rigid authoritarian viewpoint. Even communists, who were the ultimate leftists, were often called fascist by the Western press. Eventually the word developed such a bad flavor that even those who held traditional fascist beliefs disavowed the term.

Then, in the 1980s, a new generation of fascists—neofascists—came on the world scene. The main reasons for the resurgence of fascism were tough economic times and an increasingly mobile Third World population that, in the view of some Western Europeans, threatened the racial "purity" of their nations. All over Europe, and in America as well, images of the old fascist regimes came to life again. Shouts of *Sieg Heil*, swastikas, straight-arm salutes, fire bombings, and the murder of innocent people—there is nothing very new about these fascists. They spout the same hatred and use the same violent tactics of Mussolini's original group, but they usually lack a comprehensive political agenda.

Perhaps the only thing new about the neofascists is the willingness of some of them to embrace the much-maligned term. "We follow a policy that we hope will regain lost values in our community," one Italian neofascist leader told *Time* magazine in June 1994. "Fascism is the family, respect for older people and for the fatherland." Others with decidedly neofascist leanings prefer to distance themselves from the word. "If we were in the U.S. we'd be called Republicans," argues Gianfranco Fini, leader of Italy's National Alliance (formerly the openly fascist Italian Socialist Movement).

Thus the definition of neofascist depends on who's talking. Neofascists are right-wing, but at what point does someone cross the line from being conservative to being neofascist? The most visible neofascists are those with shaved heads and raised palms. But smooth, diplomatic politicians like Fini may in the end be Mussolini's most effective flag bearers.

WHAT'S A COUP D'ÉTAT? WHAT'S A JUNTA?

Coup d'état—or coup, for short—is a French phrase meaning "stroke (or blow) of state." In political terms, a coup is the unconstitutional seizure of governmental power by a small group, usually with the help of the military. The prime elements in a successful coup are planning, surprise, and the ability to apply force if necessary. Violence is certainly possible, but it doesn't occur in every coup (nonviolent takeovers are called *bloodless coups*). Often a coup is so swift and complete that the citizenry doesn't have time to respond. Since the army is usually on the side of the coup, the general population is often hesitant to defy the new order.

What makes a coup different from a revolution? A coup takes place at the top of a government, while a revolution is born across a wide spectrum of the population. Napoleon Bonaparte carried off one of the first modern coups in 1799, when he convinced the governing councils of the First French Republic that Jacobeans were threatening their power. He had the council members meet in a French suburb, then rallied his soldiers, dissolved the entire council, and established himself as dictator of France. More recent coups have been just as speedy: It took Fulgencio Batista y Zaldívar less than ninety minutes to grab power in Cuba in 1952.

In Latin America, where coups have become almost a tradition, the group that comes into power following a coup is usually referred to by the media as the "ruling junta." *Junta* is a Spanish word meaning "a council or committee created to control the government." A junta can gain power by revolution or by coup; the point is that a junta is not elected, but seizes power. For a long while American broadcasters insisted on pronouncing the *j* in the English fashion (like the *j* in jelly). The correct pronunciation is *hoon*-tah.

WHAT IS A JIHAD?

In the Islamic faith, a *jihad* is a "holy war" undertaken to expand Islam into new territories or to defend it. Because the political organization that calls itself the Islamic Jihad has had a very high profile over the past decade or so, many in the West assume that the actions taken by the Islamic Jihad accurately reflect the Islamic concept of jihad. Such is not the case. A genuine jihad, one that meets the requirements set down by Islamic law, has rarely been invoked since the earliest ages of the faith, when Islam was battling the Meccans for survival.

There are many criteria that must be met before a jihad can rightfully be supported by religious leaders. First, there must be a reasonable chance of winning the conflict. If there is not, the jihad should not be undertaken. A jihad is illegal unless its purpose includes bringing unbelievers to the faith. When these unbelievers have either accepted Islam or agreed to exist in accordance with its laws, the jihad must cease. Similarly, if the jihad was undertaken in response to a threat, it must cease once the threat subsides. Not all young men are required to take part in a jihad, only enough of them to ensure a likely victory.

WHAT IS THE INTIFADA?

Intifada is the Arabic word for "uprising." Since December 9, 1987, it has come to mean the Palestinian uprising that began on that day in the Gaza Strip section of Israel. Palestinian protests, which grew into a series of violent demonstrations against Israeli soldiers, were a response to the shooting death of a Palestinian girl by an Israeli settler a month earlier. Palestinian youths sparked the intifada when they ambushed a group of Israeli soldiers and began pelting them with stones. The stone throwing escalated as the days went on, and soon the violence spread to other parts of the West Bank. Eventually the Israelis opened fire on the crowd and killed several Palestinians. Over the next two years, more than eight hundred Palestinians and forty-four Israelis died in the conflict. The intifada marked a turning point in the international perception of the situation in Israel, and triggered a chain of events that led to the return of Jericho and the Gaza Strip to the Palestinians in 1994.

WHAT'S THE DIFFERENCE BETWEEN A MULLA AND AN AYATOLLAH?

A *mulla* is an Iranian term for a religious scholar, dignitary, or jurist. The word is used throughout other parts of Asia as well as in Iran, and means "master." An *ayatollah* is several large rungs up the ladder from a mulla. How *ayatollah* got there is an interesting tale.

Although the word *ayatollah* also has its roots in Iran, these roots are surprisingly shallow. The ayatollah is a twentieth-century invention of the Shiite Muslim sect; ayatollahs didn't exist in traditional Islamic cultures. The concept of the ayatollah arose in the 1920s, the fruit of a conflict between two different schools of Islamic thought. The ayatollah group, who won the power struggle, felt that mujtahids (religious authorities a step up from mullas) were obligated to make original decisions of canon law; that is, they were duty bound to interpret Islamic teachings on a daily basis.

What gave the movement real impact was not merely the idea of interpreting canon law. After all, anyone can interpret anything he likes in the privacy of his own home. But who would listen to the mujtahid's proclamations? Another edict answered this question. The new doctrine taught that every Shiite must be a follower of a particular mujtahid. Dead mujtahids didn't count—Shiites had to choose a living mujtahid and obey his teachings. The mujtahids received religious taxes, similar to tithings, from their followers. Lesser mullas also had to pledge allegiance to a mujtahid.

Mujtahids had existed before this period, but with the new doctrine in place, the number of mujtahids quickly mushroomed. Those with especially large followings decided to give themselves a raise in rank: They would now be called *hujjat al-Islam,* or "proof of Islam." All well and good—until *their* number swelled so much that yet another title had to be created for the most powerful Hujjat al-Islams. This title was *ayatollah,* "Divine Spirit."

It didn't stop there. Soon there were so many ayatollahs that a new title was created: *Ayatollah al-'Uzma,* "the greatest

sign of God." After the 1979 Revolution in Iran, the Ayatollah Khomeini gave up using "ayatollah" altogether and
took the title of "imam." This is the ultimate name. It means
"messiah" and refers to one who is the true successor to
Mohammed.

CAN ANYONE FORM A CARTEL?

Not in the United States—supposedly. A cartel is basically a
monopoly, and monopolies are technically illegal in the
United States. Cartels are formed by groups of businesses or
by nations, the goal being to control prices and production
within a particular market. The most famous cartel is OPEC
(Organization of Petroleum Exporting Countries). The thirteen OPEC nations fix prices of the crude oil they export and
agree upon the quantities each country will produce. Other
cartels abound—coffee cartels, airline cartels; the Philippines
even had a coconut oil cartel. But although antitrust laws
forbid U.S. companies from fixing prices and setting production quotas, cartels sometimes prove difficult to resist.

Take the case of aluminum. In June 1994 *The Wall Street
Journal* described the birth of an international aluminum cartel in which the U.S. plays a key role. Of course, "all of the
participants are shocked—*shocked*—that anyone would call
it a cartel," reported the *Journal*. Nevertheless, price and production rates were set by the group, whose members call the
agreement a "two-year memorandum of understanding."

Why did the Justice Department allow U.S. companies to
join the group? It seems that the former Soviet Union was
beginning to dump huge amounts of aluminum onto the
world market. In the old days, half of their vast aluminum
resources went to the Soviet military complex. With that ka-
put, Russian aluminum producers were frantic to get rid of
their metal. As they exported more and more of it, prices

dropped worldwide. Suddenly it became expedient for everyone, including both Russian and U.S. aluminum producers, to join together to set prices and regulate output. With a cadre of antitrust lawyers hovering over the procedures, the two-year pact was ironed out. If it works, experts say, Russia will probably pressure the United States to form similar "noncartels" for steel, aerospace products, petrochemicals, and electronics.

WHAT IS THE DOW?

The Dow—short for Dow Jones industrial average—is an index of the average closing prices of thirty blue-chip stocks. There are more than 6,700 stocks in the market, but the Dow, with its thirty stocks, is used to gauge and forecast the health of the economy.

How does the Dow work? It began simply enough in 1884, when financial journalist Charles Henry Dow devised a way to help his readers track the fluctuations in the market. He chose eleven stocks—mostly railroads—and added up the closing price of one share of each company's stock. Then he divided by 11 to come up with an average. In 1928 Dow added another nineteen industrial companies to the list. The editors of the *Wall Street Journal* (which is owned by Dow Jones & Co.) substitute new companies for the originals only if a business changes drastically, merges, or goes bankrupt. That's happened just seventeen times in the past sixty-six years.

But other changes in the financial landscape have affected the Dow, and some experts question its worth as an accurate gauge of the market. One complaint is that about 80 percent of the country's workforce is employed by service industries, yet about 80 percent of the Dow is made up of stocks for manufacturing, not service, companies. That means the bulk of America's industry is underrepresented by the Dow. Another problem lies in the Dow's size. Because it contains only thirty stocks, a strong move by any one of them can skew the index. How? Because the Dow is based on the closing price of a single share of a company's stock, not the market value of the entire company. The result: Small companies with high-priced shares can have a greater effect on the Dow's average than huge companies with many more lower-priced shares—even though the big company may be more profitable than the small one. For these reasons and more, few financial professionals use the Dow in research. Yet they all continue to quote it. The Dow is ingrained in Wall Street culture and is recognized and basically understood by everyone in the field.

WHAT'S THE DIFFERENCE BETWEEN THE NEW YORK, TOKYO, AND PACIFIC STOCK EXCHANGES?

Aside from their respective geographical locations, the main difference lies in what kinds of stocks are traded on each, and what hours they are traded.

The New York Stock Exchange (NYSE) and the American Stock Exchange (AMEX) are the two principal stock markets in the United States. The Pacific Stock Exchange is one of fourteen smaller regional exchanges scattered across the nation. In order for a stock to be listed on the NYSE, it must meet certain criteria, for example, pretax earnings of $2.5 million and 1.1 million shares publicly held. AMEX stocks represent smaller, less financially strong companies, and the AMEX has slightly less stringent requirements: pretax income of $750,000 and 500,000 shares publicly held. Both the NYSE and the AMEX also trade the stock of foreign corporations. Companies that are too small for either get traded on the regional exchanges, such as the Pacific, Midwest, and Boston stock exchanges. All of the smaller exchanges are linked with the two in New York to facilitate buying and selling.

Many stocks—in fact, the majority of U.S. stocks—are not traded on any stock exchange but on an electronic marketplace called the Over-the-Counter Market, or OTC. The OTC is made up of brokers all over the country who trade via computers and telephone. These brokers belong to the National Association of Securities Dealers (NASD). OTC stocks are listed in the newspaper under the "NASDAQ" (National Association of Securities Dealers Automated Quotations) heading.

The stock exchange in Tokyo—as well as those in London, Sydney, Hong Kong, and other major cities worldwide—trades stock generated in those particular countries. It also trades the stock of foreign corporations that qualify to be included in those markets. There are 142 stock exchanges around the world, and worldwide trading, aided by computers, has radically quickened the pace of the market.

Stocks have always been traded twenty-four hours a day, in dozens of different countries in various time zones. London's stock exchange is the oldest, founded in 1773. Paris came next, in 1802, followed by Tokyo in 1818 and Sydney in 1872. But although many of the major exchanges have existed for more than a century, it's only recently that these markets have become closely linked to one another. There are two main reasons for this: the growing number of multinational companies that trade globally and the advent of electronic trading systems.

Because there is always a market operating somewhere in the world, a stock that is listed on several exchanges worldwide may close at one price in New York and open there the next day at a different price. In between, the stock may have been traded in Tokyo, Hong Kong, Johannesburg, or any number of places. The information and money changes hands and flies nonstop around the globe, following the clock. The result is that all markets have become much more sensitive to the economies of other nations.

WHAT ARE BEAR AND BULL MARKETS?

Don't feel like you're the last on the block to know. When people were canvassed for this book, this question was asked more than any other. A rising market is a bull market; when stock prices fall, it is a bear market. You can remember which is which by thinking of the way each animal attacks: Bears swipe their paws downward, bulls toss their horns upward.

The terms have a lively frontier history. Bearskin jobbers were famous for selling the animals' skins before the bears had actually been trapped. In the stock market, a person who sold shares in a stock he didn't own came to be known as a bear. The bear would scan the market for a stock he felt was about to drop in price. He'd arrange to sell shares of the stock at a certain price, then he'd wait for the stock to drop, buy at the new, lower price, and turn around and sell it at the previously agreed-upon higher price. This gambit depended on the stock's price dropping, and thus a bear market became a market headed downward.

The bull market probably got its name simply as the opposite of bear. The two animals were connected in the public mind because both were used in the quaint popular sports of bull and bear baiting.

WHAT IS THE FED? AND WHAT DOES IT DO?

The Fed is short for *Federal Reserve System*, our nation's national bank. Most countries have a national bank that helps stabilize their internal financial systems, but the Fed is unusual in that it is composed of twelve separate banks. It's run by a seven-member board of governors appointed by the president and confirmed by the Senate. The Fed's chairman, who serves a four-year term, is chosen by the president. Not surprisingly, presidents tend to choose chairmen who share their economic philosophy. The Fed is *not* the same as the FDIC (Federal Deposit Insurance Corporation), which insures depositors against losses up to $100,000.

The Fed was created by Congress in the early part of this century, in reaction to a banking scare. Back then—before the days of the FDIC—there used to be "runs" on banks. Some event would trigger uneasiness in bank customers, and they'd all try to withdraw their money at once. It was first come, first serve, so everyone would run to the bank to get in line. In 1907 a huge run on the banks brought the U.S. economy to the brink of disaster, until J. P. Morgan imported $100 million in gold from Europe and restored stability to the system. In 1913 Congress created the Federal Reserve so it wouldn't have to rely on the kindness of magnates to ensure economic stability.

Technically the Fed is a corporation owned by banks, not a government agency, though it operates much the same as one. We most often hear about the Fed when it is about to raise or lower interest rates (*see below*). The main purpose of the Fed is to set economic policy and supervise banking operations. Among other duties, the Fed:

✳ LENDS MONEY TO MEMBER BANKS. The interest it charges is called the *discount rate*. This is what newscasters are referring to when they announce that "the Fed raised interest rates today." Why is this number watched so closely? Because the *prime interest rate* is based on the discount rate. The prime interest rate is the rate banks charge their best customers. The average citizen's interest rate is always higher than the prime.

✳ HANDLES THE BANKING BUSINESS OF THE U.S. GOVERN-MENT. The Fed gets our tax money, writes our unemployment, social security, and other government checks, and authorizes payment on Treasury bills, notes, and bonds.

✳ REGULATES THE FLOW OF MONEY INTO THE ECONOMY. It does this by buying and selling government securities. The goal: Keep the value of the dollar stable.

✳ CONTROLS CURRENCY. When bills and coins get worn, the Fed takes them out of circulation and directs the Treasury Department to issue new money.

✳ AUDITS BANKS. The Fed monitors banks to make sure bank officials are following regulations and lending money in a legal and prudent fashion.

✳ GUARDS THE GOLD. The New York Federal Reserve bank contains roughly ten thousand tons of gold. The Fed administers the exchange of this gold bullion between countries.

✳ CLEARS THE CHECKS. More than fifteen billion checks pass through the Fed each year, as it facilitates the speedy transaction of funds between banks.

How does the Fed distribute its money? Each of the twelve banks that comprise the Fed controls some of the money. In all, they have twenty-five regional branches spread across the nation. If you're curious about where your money comes from, examine a dollar bill: To the left of the president's portrait you'll see a round Federal Reserve Bank emblem with a letter in it. That letter, along with the number that appears in the four corners of the bill, signifies the branch that issued the money. The seal also names the city where the bill originated.

WHAT ARE HOUSING STARTS?

Housing starts refers to the number of building permits issued in a given period of time, generally one month. A healthy economy usually generates a demand for new housing, so when housing starts are "up" it's taken as a good sign. Newscasters tend to mention housing starts frequently because they are one of the eleven *leading economic indicators*, and housing is easier for the public to relate to than some of the other indicators, such as stock prices or the *M2 Money Supply* (see below).

WHAT IS THE INDEX OF LEADING ECONOMIC INDICATORS?

Don't let your eyes glaze over—only people who already know what the Index is are allowed to turn the page. Government economists calculate the Index every month, and it is duly reported on the evening news. Hearing that "the Index of Leading Economic Indicators is up again for the third straight month" should make you shout with glee, since three consecutive rises in the Index officially means that the economy is hopping; three consecutive drops means it is faltering.

If the monthly Index hasn't got you on the edge of your seat, maybe it's because you don't realize the wealth of information it reflects. The Index is based on eleven indicators. Several of them measure manufacturing performance. Stock prices are also measured, as is the total amount of liquid cash readily available to Americans, which is called the *M2 Money Supply*. Four indicators pop up most often on the nightly news. One is housing starts, described above. *Jobless claims* is another important indicator—these are the number of new applications for unemployment insurance. More jobless claims means more people are out of work. *Durable goods* is an indicator that measures the backlog of orders for manufactured items; a continued backlog signals a continued demand. Finally, a rise in *new factory orders* means more people are buying goods—another positive sign. Put them all together and you've got one heck of an Index. Now are you impressed?

Skipped History

❊   ❊   ❊

WHEN WERE THE STONE AGE, THE BRONZE AGE, AND THE IRON AGE?

Archeologists trace the evolution of humans by the materials they used to make tools and weapons. This is called the "Three Ages System." There aren't any strict cutoffs, because the three basic ages—stone, bronze, and iron—overlapped one another.

The Stone Age began about a million years ago and ended around 3000 B.C., but many parts of the world technically were still in the Stone Age in the fifteenth century. As late as the 1700s, some aboriginal groups were using Stone Age techniques of toolmaking. Even today stories crop up every now and then about Stone Age tribes living in some forgotten jungle, but these tales must be taken with a grain of salt.

The Bronze Age, like the Stone Age, doesn't refer to a specific period of time but to a phase of development when humans began to fashion bronze tools. In Mesopotamia the Bronze Age began around 3000 B.C.; Europeans didn't catch on until 1800 B.C. Some areas—most notably, Africa south of the Sahara—skipped the Bronze Age altogether and went directly to iron. Around 1100 B.C. the people of Asia Minor began working with iron, officially heralding the start of the Iron Age.

The end of the Iron Age is even more unclear than the other two. *The Facts on File Dictionary of Archaeology* explains that "usage varies from area to area: in much of Europe, for instance, the Iron Age is taken to end with the expansion of the Romans, while in parts of Africa the Iron Age continues until the colonial era." Technically speaking, the Iron Age should last at least until the Industrial Revolution. "We could regard ourselves as still in the Iron Age today," says the *Dictionary*, "but traditionally the term is not used in this way."

As more advanced archeological techniques allow scientists a better view of the species' past, the overlap among the ages becomes more apparent. Because of this, the Three Ages System is becoming obsolete. But the system is far superior to what came before it, which was nothing—all of so-called prehistory was lumped together in an undifferentiated blur. Tracing a culture's development by its tools and weapons has proven to be a valid and immensely useful approach. For all its drawbacks, no one has come up with a better way.

What did the Rosetta Stone decipher?

The Rosetta Stone provided the link between ancient Egyptian hieroglyphics and Greek writing. The basalt stone, measuring 3¾ feet high and 2½ feet wide, dates from 196 B.C. It was discovered in 1799, and it took three scholars working successively for more than thirty years to determine the basic principles of hieroglyphic writing. The Rosetta Stone wasn't intended to be a translation tool; it was a decree honoring Ptolemy V Epiphanes, written in three types of script. At the top of the stone the decree is written in hieroglyphics. In the center of the stone the decree is repeated in a script of spoken

Egyptian, and at the bottom it is repeated again in Greek. Because the Rosetta Stone is nearly intact, scholars of written Greek were able to translate the Greek portion, and based on the translation, to decipher the hieroglyphics. One especially exciting aspect of the endeavor was the discovery that hieroglyphics were largely alphabetic, not just pictorial. They actually spelled words, and didn't merely represent ideas through pictures, as had previously been thought.

WHAT'S THE DIFFERENCE BETWEEN THE DARK AGES AND THE MIDDLE AGES?

The term *Dark Ages* was originally coined by Renaissance intellectuals during the sixteenth century. They considered the thousand-year period between the fall of the Roman Empire and their own era to be one long "Gothic night," as Renaissance writer François Rabelais put it.

The Dark Ages now are usually considered to be the five hundred years between the fifth and tenth centuries. It was during this period that Europe was at its most chaotic. In the years following the collapse of Roman rule around A.D. 470, groups of Huns, Goths, Vandals, Jutes, Angles, Saxons, Vikings, and others swarmed over the Continent vying for power and territory (and inspiring a whole industry of board games). One reason the Dark Ages seem so dark to us now is that little written history from that period survives to enlighten us. At that time the Christian Church was the sole cohesive cultural force, and monasteries were busy trying to preserve the works of ancient Greece and Rome. Intent on this effort, they all but ignored their own world.

Most historians consider the Middle Ages to encompass the Dark Ages. The Middle Ages are the period between ancient and modern times, beginning with the fall of Rome and ending with the Renaissance. The word *medieval* refers to anything relating to the Middle Ages. Although Renaissance dwellers looked down upon medieval ideas and customs, the era contributed enormously to the civilization of Europe: the Cathedral at Chartres, illuminated manuscripts, and the poetry of Geoffrey Chaucer are all products of the Middle Ages.

WHO WERE THE GREGORIANS? WHY DID THEY CHANT AND DEVELOP CALENDARS?

First things first: the Gregorians weren't a "they." Anything named after a Pope Gregory is called *Gregorian*. Gregorian chants were named after Pope Gregory I, known as Gregory the Great. The Gregorian calendar was named for its creator, Pope Gregory XIII.

Chants, or plainsong, existed since the earliest days of Christianity, long before Pope Gregory I was elected in 590. Gregorian chants have several unique characteristics: They consist of a single melodic line, they are sung unaccompanied, and they usually have a rhythm that is free, not divided into regular patterns. Chants grew out of the music Jewish cantors brought to the traditional feast held on Sabbath days. From these songs blossomed a wealth of liturgical chants in a number of different traditions, from Byzantinian to Gallican to Old Roman. Gregory the Great was a big promoter of liturgical chanting in Rome, and eventually the whole body of Roman chanting was named after him.

Nearly a thousand years after Gregory the Great died, Pope Gregory XIII held the position of pontiff. Together with an astronomer, Christopher Clavius, Gregory in 1582 created the Gregorian calendar, which is used worldwide today. What prompted Gregory to improve on the Julian calendar, which was then in use? The bane of all previous calendar makers: leap year. Astronomers everywhere had tried to wrest the lunar/solar year into a regular pattern, but it confounded them all.

The Julian calendar almost got it right. In an attempt to make up for past errors, Julius Caesar decreed that the year 46 B.C. would have 445 days. Every year thereafter would have 365, with each fourth year getting an extra day. But the Julian calendar created three leap years too many in every 385-year period. Once again, important holidays based on natural phenomena (such as solstices and equinoxes) drifted away from their assigned calendar dates.

Because Easter is determined by the spring solstice, Gregory XIII was particularly concerned. He and Clavius devised the final formula that ensured the solstices would stay put. Here it is: Leap years occur in years divisible by 4. But if a year ends in 00 it must be divisible by 400 in order to be a leap year. Thus 1600 and 2000 are leap years; 1800 and 1900 are not.

WHAT, AND WHEN, WAS THE BLACK DEATH?

"No bells tolled, and nobody wept no matter what his loss because almost everyone expected death. . . . And people said and believed, 'This is the end of the world.' "
—*Agnolo di Turo, a chronicler of Sienna, Italy*

The Black Death—a combination of the bubonic and pneumonic plagues—killed one third of the human population in China, Asia, India, Europe, and Northern Africa in a scant sixteen years, from 1334 to 1350. In Europe alone, 20 million perished in two years, from 1348 to 1350. No disaster before or since has come close to the devastation wrought by the Black Death.

The bubonic plague had struck Europe before the 1300s: The earliest recorded instance was in Athens in 430 B.C. What made the Black Death different was that two types of plague occurred simultaneously. The bubonic plague, which causes swollen, black lymph glands and kills its victims within about five days, is carried by rats and fleas. The pneumonic plague is carried by rats and fleas, but infected humans, too, can spread the disease, in the same way the common cold is spread. The pneumonic plague kills its victims even faster than the bubonic—within three days, or sometimes as little as twenty-four hours.

Because it raged so fiercely and killed so swiftly, the Black Death generally settled on an area for only four to six months before burning itself out. Large cities suffered longer than rural areas. Physicians in the Middle Ages knew nothing about microscopic carriers of disease, and so had no idea what was causing or spreading the plague. They settled on "planetary influences," a contorted astrological theory that became the official scientific explanation.

What was the Children's Crusade? Where were the adults?

The Christian Crusades took place from 1096 to about 1300. The crusaders' mission was to wrest the Holy Land, specifically Jerusalem, from Muslim control and convert it to Christianity. Some crusaders had solely pious objectives; many others wanted land, money, and power from these exploits. Four major crusades had occurred before the heartrending Children's Crusade set off.

There actually were two separate Children's Crusades, instigated by two young boys. The first was sparked in 1212 by a French shepherd, Steven of Vendôme. This child persuaded thirty thousand boys and girls, many of them younger than twelve years old, to follow him to the port of Marseilles, where merchants agreed to take them to Palestine. Two of the ships sank, killing all aboard. The rest of the crusaders met an equally bad fate—they died of starvation or disease, or were sold as slaves.

A second Children's Crusade, this one about twenty thousand strong, was led by another French lad, Nicholas of Cologne. He marched his holy army across the Alps, where the majority died of exhaustion and hunger. At this point the Italian bishops and the pope finally stepped in, convincing most of the survivors to return home.

It seems astonishing that the adult population didn't try to dissuade these youngsters from their journey. But children held a very different, and much less protected, place in medieval society than they do now. By many accounts, medieval parents weren't as emotionally attached to their children as modern parents are. Some historians blame the parents' coldness on the high infant mortality rate: Emotional investment in any young child was risky. Besides, a child who died could always be "replaced" by another, since many women bore six to ten children and expected only three or four to survive.

Equally important in understanding the Children's Crusade is recognizing that, in the Middle Ages, the concept of childhood was very limited. In *The Disappearance of Childhood*, Neil Postman recounts that "in all the sources, one finds that in the Middle Ages childhood ended at age seven. Why seven? *Because that is the age at which children have command over speech*." Postman believes that the near-total illiteracy of people in the Middle Ages, and their reliance on oral communication, resulted in the blurring of the line between childhood and adulthood. Everyone lived together, slept together, worked together. No adult secrets were kept from children. In the sixteenth century, "the printing press created a new definition of adulthood *based on reading competence,* and, correspondingly, a new concept of childhood *based on read-*

ing incompetence. Prior to the coming of that new environment, infancy ended at age seven and adulthood began at once. There was no intervening stage because none was needed." (The italics are Postman's.)

A typical ten-year-old boy either would have gone to work as a laborer or, if he was lucky enough to go to school (where everything was taught orally), "would have lived on his own in lodgings in the town, far from his family. It would have been common for him to find in his class adults of all ages, and he would not have perceived himself as different from them." And Postman concludes that, "immersed in an oral world, living in the same social sphere as adults . . . the seven-year-old male was a man in every respect except for his capacity to make love and war."

In light of this, it's a little easier to comprehend why children would have decided to set out across a continent on their own and why so many parents would have let them go.

WHAT WAS THE REFORMATION?

The Reformation is the name given to the period of time when the Catholic Church splintered into various Protestant factions. It was a religious rebellion that spanned Europe and had a profound impact on Western civilization, sparking brutal conflicts and ultimately laying the groundwork for the **Enlightenment** (see page 32) and the modern age (see also **Postmodernism**, page 216).

It began at the dawn of the sixteenth century. The Roman Catholic Church was at that time the only church, interpreting the Bible for all Christians and insisting that only clergy had the right to do so. It was on this point that the people rebelled. Two hundred years earlier an English priest, John Wycliffe, had announced that all Christians should be able to interpret the Bible as they saw fit. Wycliffe's followers translated the Latin Bible into English and distributed the new Bibles throughout the land. In the early 1500s a Saxon monk named Martin Luther put Wycliffe's ideas into action by directly opposing the pope.

Luther attacked the church for selling indulgences that in essence allowed people to buy pardons for their sins without actually having to repent. He rejected the pope's authority and declared that the only true Christian authority was the Bible itself. The vows taken by nuns and monks, the celibacy of the clergy, the church's monasteries—Martin Luther disdained them all. In 1520, when Pope Leo X wrote a papal bull condemning Luther and excommunicating him, the priest burned it along with a copy of the church's canon law.

Although it was greatly displeased with Martin Luther, the Church didn't immediately appreciate the chord he had struck with European Christians. Within ten years of the papal bull incident, the movement—now officially dubbed Protestantism—had caught on like wildfire. The flames were fanned by the Church's continued attempt to dominate the Holy Roman Empire, which at that time was basically composed of German states. The Holy Roman emperor, Charles V (a German), fought various German and French factions in the name of the church, which infuriated the citizens of those countries who wanted independence from Rome. Elsewhere in Europe—in Holland, Switzerland, and France—and in England, determined Protestants turned the Reformation into an unstoppable wave.

In England, the king himself—Henry VIII—ruptured the ties to Rome. When the pope refused to annul Henry's marriage to Catherine of Aragon, Henry forced parliament to pass acts declaring that the pope had no authority in England and establishing the Church of England as an entity separate from Rome. Henry, who eventually married six times, made himself head of the church. To this day Great Britain's ruling monarch heads the Church of England.

By 1545 Rome realized the depth of the Protestants' feelings and passed a number of decrees intended to right itself in the eyes of Christians: It curtailed abuses and placed renewed emphasis on ancient teachings, rituals, and traditions. Rome won back half the people it had lost to Protestantism, but Europe remained from that point on divided between Catholics and various denominations of Protestants.

WHAT WAS THE ENLIGHTENMENT?

On June 23, 1633, Galileo Galilei officially recanted his previous claim that the sun, not the Earth, was the center of solar system. His action demonstrated the anguish caused to the Church by the Enlightenment, an intellectual movement of the seventeenth and eighteenth centuries based on the belief that the universe and humankind can be understood through pure reason. Also called the Age of Reason and the Age of Rationalism, the Enlightenment overturned the Christian worldview that had dominated Western philosophy for more than a thousand years.

Ancient Greek philosophers, particularly Aristotle, had observed the regularity of the natural world and concluded that they made sense logically and that the human mind could understand these patterns. Christianity opposed this view, insisting that reason and logic could be employed only if they fell in line with God's word. The parts of God's word that didn't make sense rationally were to be taken on faith. Throughout the Middle Ages Christianity held sway, and intellectual reasoning gave way to Christian doctrine. The Renaissance saw a renewal in classical teachings, and the **Reformation** (see page 30) saw the splintering of the church, both of which opened the door for a return to logic as a way of interpreting the world. Finally, the scientific advances of the sixteenth and seventeenth centuries, led by men such as Copernicus, Galileo, and Sir Isaac Newton, struck at the very heart of the church's belief system.

The rationalists had opinions about every aspect of society, not just religion and science. But because so many of the areas rationalists attacked—social structures, politics, law, history—trampled ground that was controlled by the church, religious leaders were extremely intolerant of all who, like Galileo, took issue with biblical text. The rationalists themselves were rarely atheists; most considered themselves deists, which meant that they believed in a supreme being who set the universe in motion, but not in the God of the Old or New Testament.

What were the basic tenets of the Enlightenment? The belief that certain natural laws guide the actions of humans everywhere, no matter the culture or race. The concept of universal brotherhood, and the abhorrence of slavery and brute force to control the populace. Most rationalists believed that a monarchy was the natural form of rule, but others, including John Locke, laid the foundations of a new system, democracy. Rationalist Adam Smith developed the basic ideas of capitalism, arguing that government should not interfere with the economy but should let the natural flow of the free market regulate itself. Perhaps the most revolutionary aspect of the Enlightenment was its faith in the human mind and its optimistic view of the future. The era's scientific breakthroughs, combined with the explosion of new ideas in all areas of life, led to a widespread feeling that humanity was on an unimpeded march forward, progressing exactly as fast as Enlightenment thinkers could work out rational explanations for the world.

Although many of the core beliefs of the Enlightenment

are still deeply ingrained in our worldview, it became apparent in the late 1700s that rationalism had some serious shortcomings. Reason could not explain all human actions; people are propelled not only by their intellect but by their passions, their desires, their will—even their faith. Emotional, irrational human beings charge through history heedless of how, rationally speaking, they ought to behave. The great philosophers Immanuel Kant and David Hume both finally concluded that human nature cannot be explained by reason alone. Inevitably, rationalism was challenged by a new philosophy called Romanticism, which valued the irrational, the natural world, subjectivity, and individuality.

WHAT WAS ROMANTICISM?

The Romantic period took place from 1770 to 1850, but its theories continue to influence modern thought. Our belief in individual freedom and the possibilities of the self can be traced to Romanticism. Toward the end of the 1700s, **Rationalism** (see the **Enlightenment**, page 32) gave way to this new philosophy. Romanticism was not so much a revolt against the Age of Reason as it was an attempt to reconcile it with the more intuitive aspects of human experience. The romanticists rejected the notion that the world can be understood solely through reason, but they didn't forsake the positive parts of Rationalism, for instance, rigorous scientific exploration. Instead, they tried to enlarge Rationalism into a philosophy that also valued spirituality, diversity, and feeling.

The movement grew especially strong after the French Revolution of 1789, when all previous modes of thinking were swept aside. Building a new society required passion, and unlike the rationalists, romanticists embraced religious faith—the more intensely felt, the better. Romanticists encouraged cultural nationalism as opposed to the cosmopolitan attitudes of the Enlightenment. The point wasn't to prove one nation's superiority over another (that type of racialism hadn't yet taken hold) but to rediscover historical roots. Romantic thinkers held nature in awe, viewing it as the pure, almost mystical opposite to the harsh and ugly world of urban civilization. Most important, Romanticism prized the individual and human creativity. Jean-Jacques Rousseau, called the father of Romanticism, believed that in their natural state, unsullied by civilization, men and women could cultivate their hearts and instinctively understand the deepest truths about life.

DID THE THREE MUSKETEERS ACTUALLY EXIST?

Only in the mind of Alexandre Dumas, the Elder. He wrote the novel *The Three Musketeers* in 1844. The setting is France in about 1625, and the musketeers—Athos, Porthos, and Aramis—are swordsmen who serve King Louis XIII. Together they defeat Cardinal Richelieu and his agent, Lady de Winter (who happens to be Athos' wife), in their plot to embarrass the royal family. The confusion about whether the musketeers were real arises because Louis XIII and Richelieu did indeed exist. But as many authors have done, Dumas used historical figures as foils for his fictional creations.

WHAT WERE THE FIRST AND SECOND REICHS?

Everyone knows about Hitler's Third Reich—but what were the first two?

The First Reich—*Reich* is the German word for "kingdom" or "empire"—was what Hitler only dreamed his Germany would become: a powerful collection of unified German states. Also known as the Holy Roman Empire, the First Reich lasted more than eight hundred years. Why were German states called the Holy *Roman* Empire? It has to do with the political landscape of Europe during the reign of Otto the Great, who united Germany.

In the tenth century the church controlled about a third of the land in Otto's Germany, part of an ever-changing church-dominated territory that would come to be called the Holy Roman Empire. The church in Rome was attempting to unify Western Europe against the Byzantine Empire of Eastern Europe. But without a common language, shared traditions, or a unified system of government, the "Empire" was a papal conceit more than a true region.

Because the popes spent much time and energy vying with kings for the control of Europe, their attention to spiritual matters waned. Most church officials carried on exactly like any other noblemen: They had wives, mistresses, and families. Their chief interest was in manipulating the church-held lands they controlled in Italy, Germany, and across Europe. In the hundred years before Otto entered the scene, the goings-on at the Vatican seemed more inspired by Caligula than by Christ: Twenty popes came and went, many of them murdered or deposed. Marozia, the mistress of one pope, was the mother of another.

Much of Otto's time was spent creating new bishoprics and placing his friends and family members in charge of them so he could seize control of church-owned properties. Meanwhile, Pope John XII (Marozia's son), weary of the constant intrigue, asked Otto to intervene in papal affairs. In 962 Otto crossed the Alps into Italy and intervened in the most dramatic way: He declared himself king of both Italy and Germany. John XII crowned Otto Holy Roman Emperor. Soon thereafter Otto had John XII deposed for "murder, sacrilege, and immorality."

The First Reich's grasp of Italy lasted about two hundred years. By the end of the 1200s the Holy Roman Empire had shrunk—even parts of Germany were not under the emperor's control. Still, Germany's kings called themselves "Holy Roman Emperor" and referred to their territory as the Holy Roman Empire until Napoleon defeated them in 1806.

The Second Reich was a much briefer affair. It was the creation of Otto von Bismarck, who became chancellor of Prussia in 1862 and five years later helped organize the North German Federation, a collection of more than three dozen states. This configuration survived until the last German kaiser was overthrown in 1918. The Second Reich had lasted a mere forty-seven years.

Hitler boasted that his Third Reich would last one thousand years. Fortunately, he was 988 years short of the mark.

WHAT DOES IT MEAN TO "MEET YOUR WATERLOO"?

Napoleon Bonaparte met his in 1815, and since then, to "meet your Waterloo" has come to mean to endure your final, irrevocable defeat.

Napoleon had been forced to abdicate power in 1814, but less than a year after he was exiled to an island off the coast of Italy, he returned to Europe, gathered what remained of his loyal forces, and tried once again to seize power. At Waterloo, a small town outside Brussels, Belgium, Napoleon fought his last battle. The French fired the first shots on June 18, and in less than twenty-four hours forty thousand Frenchmen lay dead or wounded. British and Prussian troops converged on Napoleon's army and lay waste to them by night's end, suffering heavy casualties themselves—about twenty-three thousand men. After this episode, Napoleon failed to pull together another army. He was forced to abdicate power a second and final time and was exiled to St. Helena, a bleak island off the west coast of Africa, where he eventually died.

WHERE IS THE MASON-DIXON LINE?

At 39°43' 26.3" north latitude. The line was established by two British surveyors, Charles Mason and Jeremiah Dixon, to settle a boundary feud between the Penn family of Pennsylvania and the Calvert clan of Maryland. History books state that it took the surveyors four years to stake out the line, from 1763 to 1767. In 1769 the Crown approved the boundary, and in 1784 the line was extended to its full length: It marks the boundaries of Pennsylvania on the north and Delaware, Maryland, and West Virginia on the south.

The Mason-Dixon Line became prominent in the American consciousness in the years prior to the Civil War, when it became the dividing line between slave and free states. It's still used to signify the boundary between the North and the South.

WHAT WAS THE BLACK HOLE OF CALCUTTA?

History is replete with acts so brutal they stagger the imagination, and the Black Hole of Calcutta was the site of one of them. The hole was a cell 14 feet 10 inches wide and 18 feet long, in an English fort in Calcutta, India. In 1756 the British and the French were vying for control of India; in the course of the struggle, each wooed various Indian princes with money, troops, and promises of power. Tensions mounted until an Indian prince attacked the British fort, captured its men, and forced 146 of them into the tiny cell. Heat that night was intense, and the hole had only two small windows for air. By the next morning, all but 23 of the Englishmen were dead. The British swore to avenge the deaths, and war was on. In 1761 France was ousted, and the British Empire expanded to include India.

WHAT IS THE FOURTH ESTATE? AND WHAT ARE THE FIRST, SECOND, AND THIRD ESTATES?

The first three estates signified the classes of men's activities during the feudal era in Europe, which began about A.D. 850. These activities amounted to praying, fighting, and working the land for food. Thus the first estate was the clergy, the second estate was nobility (including kings) and warriors, and the third estate was everyone else, mostly peasant farmers. Eventually the members of these estates came to be known in England as lords spiritual, lords temporal, and commons (hence the House of Lords and the House of Commons).

The concept of a fourth estate is believed to have originated in 1828, when Thomas Babington Macaulay referred to a group of news reporters as "a fourth estate of the realm." Soon the "fourth estate" was a popular nickname for members of the newspaper profession. Later its meaning expanded to include any influential aspect of English political life that was *not* the government, such as the army or the news media (radio, TV, print).

WHAT ARE LUDDITES?

If you hate the telephone, abhor anything with a liquid-crystal display, and never learned to use a computer, you may have a lot in common with the Luddites, a group vehemently opposed to the advance of technology. The Luddites' tale is a poignant one. They weren't opposed to mechanization because it offended their sensibilities; to them, it was a matter of survival.

In the early 1800s, industrialization was emerging in England. Its brought many painful changes, especially for textile workers. In the Midlands, these workers revolted. Their plight sounds distressingly familiar: Working conditions were bad and getting worse; the government did little to protect them from exploitative employers; and above all, machines were taking their jobs. New wide-frame looms were being introduced, and these looms could weave hosiery faster while being operated by fewer people (the Luddites insisted that the quality of the hosiery was poorer, too).

In 1808 a minimum-wage bill was defeated in the House of Commons, and three years later the Luddites began to appear. They named themselves after Ned Ludd, a fictional leader whom they also called King Ludd and who supposedly hailed from Sherwood Forest.

The Luddites' mission was simple: Destroy the machinery that was taking their jobs. This was relatively easy to do because the textile business in the Midlands was truly a cottage industry. Company-owned looms sat in workers' cottages and, not surprisingly, the workers weren't willing to risk their lives defending the looms against Luddite attacks. The Luddites were careful always to wear masks and to keep their identities well hidden. They enjoyed a lot of local support and for about a year made some headway in thwarting the textile manufacturers and improving workers' conditions.

In 1812 the violence escalated; several Luddites and one employer were killed, and Parliament brought down the ax. Some Luddites were hanged, others were shipped off to the colonies, and the movement faded. Meanwhile, workers in other countries had also tried to stop the march of progress, but those attempts also fizzled. French machine workers threw their wooden shoes (*sabots*) into the machines to break them; the only lasting result of their efforts was the creation of the word *sabotage*.

WHAT IS SOCIAL DARWINISM?

In 1859 Charles Darwin published *On the Origin of Species*, his landmark study of the process he called natural selection. Out of this grew a theory of social evolution called Social Darwinism. Although it is no longer taken seriously by scientists or academicians, the concept of Social Darwinism continues to reverberate at the edges of the American consciousness.

To understand Social Darwinism, you must understand Darwin's theory of natural selection. Very briefly, it states that

* New species appear.
* These new species have evolved from older species.
* Evolution is the result of natural selection.
* Natural selection depends on variety.

Variations must be maintained, even in the face of nature's tendency to eliminate weaker forms of life. Thus, the strongest species survive and eventually evolve into new species—natural selection.

Darwin believed that natural selection is basically a competition among individuals for limited resources, be it food for the tiger or light for the jungle vine. The individuals that survive are superior to those that die out.

Social Darwinists applied these theories to the structure of societies: The upper classes had wealth and privilege because they were naturally superior to the lower classes. They were able to do this in part because a key puzzle in Darwin's theory had yet to be solved. This was the issue of variation. Darwin had no knowledge of genetics (although he intuited something akin to it). That left the environment—and the way individuals react to it—as the sole means by which varieties could evolve. But in fact, environment is only half the story. Consider the jungle vine that accidentally crossbreeds with another vine, creating an even stronger variety. The stronger vine is a new genetic strain. It is not stronger because it fought harder for its spot of sunlight. Therefore, there are two ways in which varieties may evolve: through genetic changes and by natural selection.

Social Darwinists didn't have to consider genetics because practically nothing was known about it. Survival of the fittest, they asserted, was the "natural" and only means by which the species evolved. If crossbreeding (in essence, chance) is left out of the equation, the fittest could survive, pass along their superior acquired traits to their offspring, and stay at the top of the evolutionary heap forever.

It wasn't hard for Social Darwinists to apply this system of evolution to human society. They simply decided that for human beings, *survival* meant ownership of property. Those who had it were superior; they had fought for and won their property (or inherited it from someone who had). The world had winners and losers; since this was natural, there was no point in trying to change it by "artificial" tactics such as redistribution of wealth or the creation of social services.

WHAT IS THE MONROE DOCTRINE?

President James Monroe introduced the Monroe Doctrine in an 1823 speech. The doctrine stated that the United States would not allow any European government to oppress, control, or otherwise interfere with any independent nation in the Western Hemisphere. It went on to say that the United States would not permit further colonization in the Americas, nor would it allow existing European colonies to extend their boarders. Its impact has waxed and waned, reflecting America's shifting relationship with other nations in the Western Hemisphere.

The doctrine began as a response to what Monroe and others at the time—including ex-presidents Jefferson and Madison—perceived as a threat from the monarchies of Russia, Austria, and Prussia to colonize parts of North America. The three European powers had vowed to put an end to representative government in Europe, and Monroe feared they might try to suppress representative government in the Americas, too. The United States also worried that Spain and France might try to regain American possessions they had earlier given up.

The doctrine was well received in America, but the European powers were scornful of Monroe's message. They had never planned a large-scale intervention anyway; what kept them from encroaching on American territory wasn't the Monroe Doctrine but America's trading partner, Great Britain. The British feared trade with the United States might be severely hampered if, for example, the now-free Spanish-American colonies suddenly were under the rule of Spain again. The powerful British navy protected America from any serious foreign threat.

As the years passed, the Monroe Doctrine shifted shapes to reflect America's political goals. Most often it has played a role—sometimes brutishly—in U.S. relations with Latin America. President Theodore Roosevelt invoked the doctrine and infused it with new life in the early 1900s. Some of the smaller American nations, he felt, were behaving in ways that might tempt European nations to interfere. If European citizens in Latin American countries were being threatened, or if their property was being taken, Roosevelt reasoned that the "mother" country might want to step in and defend its "children." With his "speak softly and carry a big stick" policy, Roosevelt decided to cut these potential interlopers off at the pass by interloping himself. Under Roosevelt, the U.S. sent armed forces into the Dominican Republic in 1905, Nicaragua in 1911, and Haiti in 1915.

President Woodrow Wilson generally continued Roosevelt's policy, although he used greater restraint. After World War I, the United States tried to mend fences with Latin America. Franklin D. Roosevelt instigated a "good neighbor" policy and introduced the concept that *all* nations in the Western Hemisphere should help support the Monroe Doctrine's goal of hemispheric security. With World War II, this security was tested by Argentina's refusal to join the Allied Powers (it remained neutral). When the other nations gathered to discuss the war and the problem with Argentina, the Monroe Doctrine was broadened to include the principle that any attack on one nation in the Western Hemisphere would be considered an attack on all. Out of this act grew the Organization of American States (OAS).

Did this newly minted brotherhood with Latin America mean the United States would stop invading other countries in its hemisphere? No. After World War II the basic premise behind the Monroe Doctrine—to protect America from outside intruders—was invoked in the fight against communist invasion. Communist movements in Latin America were perceived as threats to American security. In reaction to this, since 1954 the United States has taken action unilaterally against Guatemala, Cuba, and the Dominican Republic. It has provided military advisers to a host of other Central and South American nations, and played behind-the-scenes roles in much of the conflict that has ravaged that part of the world.

How did the Allied Powers and the Axis Powers get their names?

The *Allies* refer to nations that were allied—and victorious—in both World War I and World War II. In World War I, the Allies consisted of twenty-four countries including not only the United States, Britain, and numerous European nations, but many Central American nations and China. They fought the Central Powers—Austria-Hungary, Bulgaria, Germany, and the Ottoman Empire (now Turkey).

In World War II, the Allies expanded to include forty-nine nations. The Axis Powers comprised Bulgaria, Germany, Finland (whose primary purpose in joining the Axis was to keep the Soviet Union at bay), Hungary, Italy, Japan, and Romania, as well as some smaller nations. The Axis Powers took their name from an Italo-German decree of common interests, made in 1936. This agreement would later evolve into the 1939 "Pact of Steel," which restated Hitler's and Mussolini's mutual commitment to each other. Mussolini declared the 1936 agreement to be the axis around which other states with similar goals could collaborate.

Ironically, *Axis* was also the name Germany gave to a plan devised in July 1943 to take control of Italy. The Axis plan was inspired by Germany's belief that Italy would eventually defect to the Allied side. Indeed, in September 1943 Italy surrendered to the Allies. The German commander in charge of the area issued the code word "Axis," and proceeded to seize control of Rome. The Italian troops—a half million of them—offered virtually no resistance to the Germans, nor did they do much to aid the Allies.

What and where was the Battle of the Bulge?

The Battle of the Bulge was Germany's last great offensive of World War II. It took place in Belgium, when the Allied forces were pressing across Europe from the North Sea. On a foggy December morning in 1944, the German army launched a massive attack, twenty divisions strong. At this time the Allies had reached the German border and were stretched across Europe in a line that ran from the Netherlands to Switzerland. The German attack drove the Allies back across Belgium, creating a huge "bulge" in the Allied line. It took six weeks for the Allies to regain the upper hand, and at enormous cost to both sides: Germany lost two hundred thousand men; the Allies, sixty thousand. With this last offensive, the Nazis depleted nearly all their reserve strength, hastening their eventual defeat.

The Battle of the Bulge is the popular name for the conflict. It is officially called the Battle of Ardennes II, named for the section of Belgium where the fighting occurred. Ardennes I was fought between France and Germany in the same place during World War I.

What does the D in D-Day stand for?

Destruction . . . demolition . . . devastation? No. The *D* just stands for *D*. It's a military term that's used to designate the date of a planned action. (Similarly, the term *H-hour* designates a specific hour for a planned action.) When the date has been set, other activities related to the action can be given "D" titles, too, as in "D minus 1" for one day before the action, or "D plus 3" for three days after it. Why not just use the actual date? Because it may change, or must be kept secret, or will not be made firm until the last minute.

When most Americans think of D-Day, they're thinking

about June 6, 1944, the day the Allied forces invaded Normandy during World War II. Then there's V-E Day (Victory [in] Europe, May 8, 1945) and V-J Day (Victory [over] Japan, August 14, 1945). Because V-E and V-J actually stand for something, people assume D does too.

WHAT'S THE DIFFERENCE BETWEEN COMMUNISM AND SOCIALISM?

It's a matter of degree, at least in our modern interpretation of the words. According to the *Dictionary of Philosophy and Religion,* the two have nearly identical definitions: Communism, from the Latin *communis* ("common," "universal," "public"), is a social structure where all things are held in common. Socialism, from the Latin *socius* ("comrade"), is any association, private or public, organized around the principle of group control of property and the production and distribution of wealth. Both terms have long histories. Communism was first explored by Plato in the *Republic,* and later was advocated after the French Revolution in the latter half of the eighteenth century. The term *socialism* was first used in France in the 1830s and became a popular concept in England during that period as well.

Karl Marx took issue with socialists who advocated peaceful means—persuasion or evolution—to accomplish social change. Marx thought their view was idealistic, and he called it "Utopian Socialism." With Friedrich Engels, Marx redefined socialism, proclaiming that it is a stage through which societies must pass on their way to communism. Communism is the desired end; socialism is the means to the end. The stage of socialism is also the stage of the dictatorship of the proletariat. Lenin claimed that the Soviet Union was in the stage of socialism.

Although Marx's definitions of the two words are widely accepted, there have always been groups advocating gradual, nonviolent socialist change. In Europe, the United States, and around the world such socialist parties continue to exist. Soviet communism may have collapsed, but socialist thought, with its emphasis on cooperative societies, will probably continue to influence the political debate indefinitely.

WHAT IS THE DIASPORA?

The *Diaspora* is the term used for the Jewish community scattered around the world outside of Palestine (present-day Israel).

The first Diaspora began in biblical times, when the Babylonians conquered the Kingdom of Judah in 586 B.C. and part of the Jewish population was sold into slavery. After that, Jewish communities took root in other nations, so that by the time Jerusalem was destroyed in A.D. 70 most of the Jewish population were already part of the Diaspora. By A.D. 100, five million Jews lived outside Palestine, even though they continued to look toward it for cultural and religious leadership. Since that time, Judaism has spread across most parts of the globe, but has thrived chiefly in the Middle East, Europe, Eastern Europe, and the United States. Through the centuries, various nations have become centers of Jewish culture; some of these include Persia, Spain, France, Germany, Poland, Russia, and the United States.

The creation of a Jewish state, Israel, heightened the debate among Jewish people as to whether the Diaspora, which has tended to result in some assimilation in each host country, will doom Judaism. Some Jewish people are Zionists, who believe that only in Israel can Judaism truly flourish; others maintain that the dispersion of their people across the globe is God's will.

In recent years, the word *diaspora* also has been used when speaking of the scattering of Africans from their native land, beginning with the slave trade, although the term continues to be most strongly associated with Jewish history.

THREE

Because the Founding Fathers Said So

✳ ✳ ✳

WHAT IS A GRAND JURY?

Grand juries decide if there is enough evidence in a case to warrant a criminal trial (see also **criminal and civil suits**, page 52). "Regular" juries, called *common* or *petit* (as opposed to *grand*) juries, determine the facts in a case and acquit or convict a person for a public offense.

Grand juries are called *grand* because they are usually larger than common juries—anywhere from twelve to twenty-three people (common juries typically have twelve members). In legal lingo, a grand jury must determine "probable cause" that a crime has been committed and that a particular person ought to be tried for the crime.

The grand jury is mentioned specifically in the **Bill of Rights** (see page 72), and the founding fathers considered it an essential element of the democratic system. Its purpose: to protect individuals from unwarranted, arbitrary prosecution. The Fifth Amendment states that no one can be brought to trial for a capital crime unless a grand jury has agreed that the evidence is strong enough to warrant the trial.

The grand jury wasn't the founders' own idea. They imported it from England, where it had originated in the twelfth century. Early grand juries were almost diametrically opposed to today's version. In 1166 King Henry II decided that out of every 104 knights or "good and lawful men," twelve should be appointed to inform on the others. The members of the grand jury presented their sworn accusations to one of the king's judges—accusations that could include gossip, rumors, or events they had personally witnessed. Clearly the main idea here was not to protect citizens against unwarranted persecution. King Henry's goal was to maintain control over his subjects and property, which were greatly influenced by the church and feudal barons. The king's plan was that his grand juries would exist throughout the land, enabling him and his judges to carry out the law of the Crown no matter whose feudal territory the "crimes" occurred in.

Medieval folk accused by a grand jury were often treated to a "trial by ordeal." There were four species of ordeal: cold water, hot water, hot iron, and morsel. These were exactly as gruesome as you'd imagine. The least horrific, but just as weird and arbitrary as the others, was trial by morsel. The accused had to gulp down an ounce of bread or cheese. If he choked and grew black in the face, he was guilty; if he could swallow the morsel, he was innocent.

It took a long time for the grand jury to evolve to its current form: Five hundred years went by before grand juries asserted their independence from the Crown and won the right to hold their proceedings in secret (away from royal prosecutors). With this development, grand juries passed a major milestone, from being tools of the king to being protectors of the common man.

When British colonists came to the New World they brought with them the institution of grand juries. In the two hundred years since that time, grand juries have been both obstacles to justice and forces for good. Southern grand juries have refused to indict Ku Klux Klan members for intimidating blacks; on the other hand, grand juries have often played key roles in the fight against political corruption, as in the case of the 1872 grand jury probe of New York's Boss Tweed.

There is still a lot of argument about whether grand juries are a pointless waste of time (because they simply foreshadow what the prosecutor will do anyway) or an invaluable protector of the people. As a result of all the controversy, states vary as to how they use grand juries. Some use them only for crimes carrying death or life-term sentences; other states allow the prosecutor to decide whether or not to use a grand jury. But, as the Bill of Rights stipulates, all federal cases must be indicted by a grand jury.

WHAT DOES IT TAKE TO HANG A JURY?

It depends on the state. In many states, all it takes is one juror who is not convinced "beyond a reasonable doubt" (*not* "a shadow of a doubt") that the defendant is guilty. Some states have revised their laws so that a unanimous verdict is not necessary; instead, a majority may return a verdict. A specific number is required for the majority—it's not always seven out of twelve jurors. In these cases the number required to hang the jury varies according to jurisdiction.

WHAT IS THE DIFFERENCE BETWEEN CIVIL LAW AND CRIMINAL LAW?

Criminal law refers to actions that are crimes against the state, while civil law refers to wrongful actions one citizen commits against another person or his property. But there are many places where civil and criminal law overlap.

In *The Guide to American Law*, Richard G. Singer distinguishes between civil and criminal actions. He writes, "If A assaults and robs B, then the state may punish A for the crimes of assault and robbery, and B may sue A for damages and conversion of property." Most crimes that violate the penal code also violate the civil code. In one notorious case, a youngster accused pop star Michael Jackson of molesting him. Jackson was investigated, but there was insufficient evidence for the state to charge him with any particular crime. However, after the boy's family threatened to file a civil suit against Jackson, he settled with them rather than embark on a civil trial.

In recent years the lines between civil and criminal procedures have become especially blurred. Singer points out a few reasons for this. A basic difference between civil law and criminal law used to be that criminal law punished the perpetrator, while civil law compensated the victim. "But with the growth of statutes which require persons convicted of crime to give restitution to the victim, and the expansion of 'civil' statutes that appear to result in punishments to the defendant, the difference is less clear," he writes. What's more, punitive damages can now be awarded in civil cases. That is, the wrongdoer can be made to pay expenses beyond repayment of lost property, and these extra fines—which benefit the victim—are mostly intended to punish the perpetrator.

There are a few functional aspects of the two types of law that do make them substantially different:

* The state prosecutes a crime, while a private individual prosecutes another individual in a civil action.
* A criminal trial involves many legal protections that don't necessarily apply to a civil trial.

✻ A person can never be sent to jail for a civil action, only for a crime.

✻ A person can never lose his civil rights (for instance, the right to vote) as the result of a civil action; being convicted of a crime can result in the loss of all civil rights (including freedom or even the right to one's life).

WHAT IS THE LEGAL DEFINITION OF INSANITY?

The short answer: Being unable to comprehend the difference between right and wrong. This criteria is known as the M'Naghten test (established in 1843). But there is much more to consider, specifically, what types of mental illness allow a person legally to be considered unable to understand his or her actions. American law recognizes twenty-four forms of insanity or incompetence, any one of which may relieve a person from criminal responsibility to varying degrees, depending on the case.

Twenty-four categories of mental illness sounds like a lot, and people disagree as to which categories are reasonable. Some seem to be straightforward enough: *delirium*—when the mind acts without being directed by the will; *delusion*—a belief that something exists which, in fact, does not; and *schizophrenia*—the disintegration of the personality and loss of contact with reality. But most of the controversy about legal insanity comes from some of the other forms of insanity recognized by law. *Temporary insanity* is often used as a defense; according to *American Jurisprudence,* it is "a temporary derangement which may result from any transient condition, as, for example, intoxication." Other lesser-known varieties include *partial insanity*, *emotional insanity*, and *monomania*. With each of these, the person is entirely sane some of the time, or sort of sane all of the time, but not entirely sane all of the time. *Moral insanity* is a particularly interesting case. It is "frequently used to denote such mental disease as destroys the ability to distinguish between right and wrong in a particular act," in the words of *American Jurisprudence. Moral insanity* was also an early term for what is now called antisocial personality disorder; today a person so diagnosed is called a **sociopath** (see page 85).

One of the most hotly debated forms of insanity is *irresistible impulse.* This applies to people who know the difference between right and wrong but, because of a mental disease, cannot control their behavior. In the past, many jurisdictions allowed irresistible impulse to be added to the M'Naghten rule. In 1983, however, the American Bar Association recommended that the irresistible impulse criterion be dropped. Just two years earlier, John W. Hinckley Jr. had used the insanity plea in his defense against shooting President Ronald Reagan, spurring a wave of anti–insanity plea sentiment that led to the ABA recommendation.

WHY ARE LIBERALS TO THE "LEFT" AND CONSERVATIVES TO THE "RIGHT"?

Most historians believe that it began in France on October 1, 1791. That date marked the opening of the first French legislature after the Revolution. The assembly was packed with 745 members. As it happened, the liberal or radical members were seated to the left of the speaker, and the conservative members were seated to the right. The practice spread, and the terms *left wing* and *right wing* are still used around the world to denote the two opposing political beliefs, liberalism and conservatism.

WHAT'S THE DIFFERENCE BETWEEN A REPUBLIC AND A DEMOCRACY?

A democracy is a form of government in which a large percentage of the population participates in ruling the state. A republic is a form of government in which rulers are elected by a specific group of people who are entitled to vote. This may be a large percentage of the population, or it may not. If, for example, only people who own property are allowed to vote, and only 12 percent of the population owns property, then that republic would not be a democracy. The salient feature about a republic is that its sovereignty is not inherited; there are no kings and queens, only elected leaders. The salient features about a democracy are that its leaders are elected *and* a large percentage of the people are allowed to vote.

There are several varieties of democratic republics. In the presidential system, such as ours in the United States, the elected president acts as both head of state and head of government. In parliamentary systems, such as Germany's and Italy's, there is an elected president, but he or she does not lead the government. That duty falls to a premier or chancellor, appointed by the president and approved by a majority of members of the parliament. Some countries, such as France, have a system where an elected president and a premier share power.

What about countries such as Great Britain? Since it has a hereditary head of state—at this time, Elizabeth II—Great Britain is democratic but technically not a republic. The "ruling" monarch performs many public duties but does not actually rule the government. Great Britain has a parliamentary system, headed by a prime minister who usually is the leader of the majority party in the House of Commons.

WHY ARE DEMOCRATS SYMBOLIZED BY DONKEYS AND REPUBLICANS BY ELEPHANTS?

Both Democrats and Republicans got their mascots more than a century ago, and cartoons in the popular press were the source. In the 1800s political cartoons were scrutinized much more carefully than they are now. Their messages could be brutal and quite complex, containing several levels of meaning. Both the donkey and the elephant fit well into the dense style. Each can appear in a negative or positive light: The donkey can be stubborn and tenacious, humorous, or foolish; the elephant can be noble or clumsy, a pillar of stability or transportation for a sultan.

President Andrew Jackson was the inspiration for the first donkey. A cartoonist depicted Jackson's head on the body of a jackass. For the rest of his political life, Jackson was burdened with the jackass image. After the Civil War the donkey began to be used for other Democrats as well, and eventually it came to symbolize the party itself.

During the same post–Civil War era, Thomas Nast, senior editor of *Harper's Weekly* and the preeminent cartoonist of the day, created the Republican elephant. In a cartoon depicting his disgust with Ulysses S. Grant's scandal-ridden administration, Nast drew the Republican vote as a marauding elephant. The image was picked up by other cartoonists and soon became the Republican symbol.

Other parties have also had their beasts of burden. The Tweed political machine in New York was depicted as the Tammany Tiger, the Democrats were at one time represented by the rooster, and Theodore Roosevelt's third-party symbol was the bull moose. The Prohibitionist party had an animal, too: the camel. With all that water in its hump, it never needed a drink.

WHAT'S THE ELECTORAL COLLEGE?

Every four years at election time newscasters dutifully present an explanation of the electoral college. Baffled citizens scratch their heads and whine, "Why can't they just count the votes?" Then they promptly forget the rhyme and reason for the electoral college until next election. Here it is in a nutshell: The electoral college is the collective name for the group of electors who choose the president and vice president of the United States.

Why do we have electors, and who chooses them? It goes back to the Constitution, which was created before the development of our two-party political system. When the Constitution was being written, there was a lot of disagreement about who should elect the president and vice president. Some people wanted them to be chosen by Congress; others wanted them to be chosen by the state legislatures; still others felt it should be left to a direct vote of the people. The electoral college was the compromise developed by the authors of the Constitution.

The original idea was that the electors would be enlightened, educated men who'd calmly determine the best candidates. The people of each state would vote for their electors; in that way, the electoral college would work as a kind of indirect popular vote. In the absence of a two-party system, each elector's decision was an individual one. The Constitution instructed that each state be entitled to a number of electors equal to that state's number of senators and representatives in Congress.

In the early 1800s the two-party system began to emerge, and that changed the way the electors were chosen—and the way they voted. Each elector had to be aligned with one of the two political parties, and each made an implied pledge to vote for that party's candidate. What's made the electoral college especially mystifying is that in most states the electors themselves never appear on the ballot. By voting for a particular candidate, you are actually voting for the electors who've promised to vote for that candidate in a special joint session of Congress held in January, after the general election.

The electoral college system is winner-takes-all: The party whose candidate wins a plurality (the highest number) of a state's popular votes usually gets *all* that state's electoral votes. For instance, if Candidate Curly gets 52 percent of the popular vote in California, and Candidate Moe gets 48 percent, Curly gets *all* California's fifty-four electoral votes, not just 52 percent of them. Because of this, it's possible for a candidate to win the popular vote yet lose the electoral vote —and the election.

How can that be, if the number of electors equals the number of a state's senators and representatives? After all, every state has two senators, and the number of representatives is based on a state's population; therefore, the electoral vote should accurately reflect the will of the majority of people in a state. There's a glitch, though: the U.S. Census. It is taken at the beginning of each new decade, and each state's number of representatives is based on its population according to the census. If there's been a large shift in population, it won't be reflected in the number of representatives—and thus, electors—until the beginning of a decade. So it's conceivable that a state's population could increase drastically before the census was taken again, making its number of electors too low. Likewise, a state could lose a lot of citizens and maintain an artificially high number of electors. During election years, newscasters fill airtime trying to compute whether this phenomenon could occur enough to throw off the election. But it has happened only twice, in 1876 and 1888.

There are a total of 538 electoral votes. If there is no electoral majority in a presidential race, the decision gets "thrown to the House." At that point the House of Representatives chooses the president, with each state getting one vote. The Senate chooses the vice president in a similar manner.

The electoral college ensures the states a role in the election of the president, but because of the way it has evolved it also tends to reinforce the two-party system to the exclusion of additional parties. For that reason (among others) there have been frequent calls for its abolition. Some people think expanding our two-party system would reinvigorate U.S. politics; others argue that having three or more parties could result in the election of a president who received only a minority of the popular vote.

The debate over the electoral college is destined to linger much longer than your memory of this explanation of it. For best results, reread this entry once a month. Then amaze your friends by beating Tom Brokaw to the punch next election!

WHY ARE ELECTIONS HELD ON TUESDAYS?

If ever there was a case of "you can't please all the people all the time," here it is. In 1792 Congress mandated the first Wednesday in December as the date when the presidential electors (*see* **electoral college**, page 57) would meet to cast their votes for president and vice president. States were required to appoint their electors within the thirty-four days prior to this Wednesday. But other than that, there was no national election day; each state set its own day to appoint the electors (it would usually fall in November to comply with the thirty-four-day rule).

Appointing the electors on different days proved to be problematic. There were abuses, quite possibly the same type of abuses people object to nowadays when national election results are predicted on the East Coast before polls have closed on the West. In 1845 Congress established a national election day, the Tuesday following the first Monday in November, on which all states must appoint their electors.

Why the Tuesday following the first Monday? Because at the time, many religious people objected to traveling to the polls on Sunday, which eliminated using the first Monday of the month. (In those days getting to a polling place could mean a full day's journey.) Simply using the first Tuesday of the month wouldn't work, because it might fall on the first day of the month, which would cause problems for some businesses. Meanwhile, one hundred years later, many people resent voting on Tuesday because it's a business day. Although it's sometimes hard to get away from the job to vote, remember: Your employer is required by law to give workers time off to cast their ballots.

WHAT DOES THE VICE PRESIDENT DO?

You've seen them smashing ashtrays on talk shows, buying nasty toy dolls in Latin America, swinging golf clubs at pricey resorts. But constitutionally speaking, what is a vice president's job?

It's not much. The office was created almost exclusively as a backup for the president: the vice president takes over if the chief executive dies, resigns, is taken ill, or is impeached. Other than that, the VP has only one responsibility—to preside over the Senate and cast a tie-breaking vote if senate votes are evenly divided. Presiding over the Senate is not as impressive as it sounds. Traditionally, the VP doesn't speak at all in the Senate except to issue rulings. And senators usually take a dim view of the vice president hanging around the Senate chamber to plug the president's position on legislation, although VPs who themselves have done time in the Senate may succeed at some behind-the-scenes lobbying.

As for casting a tie-breaking vote—the opportunity for

that comes along rarely. Most wrangling over votes is done far in advance of the actual voting, and usually there is a clear majority for or against an issue. Example: In eight years as vice president, Richard Nixon cast only eight tie-breaking votes.

Until World War II, vice presidents were generally content with their limited job description, but Franklin Roosevelt's administration saw the birth of the "working" VP. Nowadays, Congress or the president gives the VP assignments that range from foreign relations to business relations to race relations. The vice president is also a member of the National Security Council. In addition, the VP recently has emerged as a sort of Charlie McCarthy figure to the president's Edgar Bergen, expressing views the president may share but dare not speak aloud; testing the water of public opinion before the prez dives in.

The obvious advantage of being vice president is that your name becomes a household word and your political value is increased many times. But it's interesting to note that, while many VPs have eyed the presidency, since 1836 only one has been elected to the highest office immediately following his stint as VP: George Bush. Eight vice presidents succeeded to the highest office upon the death of the president: John Tyler, Millard Fillmore, Andrew Johnson, Chester Arthur, Theodore Roosevelt, Calvin Coolidge, Harry Truman, and Lyndon Johnson.

WHAT IS THE CABINET?

The cabinet is composed of the heads (secretaries) of the fourteen major departments of the government. The concept is that the president should be able to use the cabinet for political advice. Cabinet members meet with the chief executive regularly and, ideally, give him thoughtful suggestions and insight into their respective arenas. This meeting of the minds rarely lives up to the ideal, however. There are plenty of reasons why it doesn't, not the least of which is that the president isn't bound by either law or tradition to pay any attention to the cabinet. Perhaps the most famous example of this is Lincoln's comment during a cabinet meeting when the entire group opposed him: "Seven nays, one aye; the ayes have it."

Cabinet members are appointed by the president, but that doesn't mean they are especially gifted, insightful, or even loyal to him. Why? Because the president's reasons for appointing the secretaries can vary widely. Some get appointed because they share his political views, some as part of a compromise with other political factions, some precisely because the president hopes they won't be too strong in their position. Certainly there also are cabinet members whom the president appoints for all the right reasons: They are intelligent individuals who can provide the chief executive with valuable information and advice.

But there's a built-in conflict each cabinet member must negotiate: He or she must advise the president *and* protect the home turf, be it defense, foreign policy, health and human services, or whatever. As the administration matures and grows more committed to specific goals, it becomes more difficult for each cabinet member to claim a big piece of the money pie. It's tricky for the secretary of defense, for example, to continue to support wholeheartedly a president who is about to cut defense funding. And the advice he'll be giving the commander in chief won't be particularly objective. If the president knows that this conflict will arise during his tenure, he may fill these touchy cabinet posts with weak individuals who won't challenge his decisions.

Despite all this, many presidents have taken office claiming to want a strong cabinet. Presidents Richard Nixon and Jimmy Carter each made a big fanfare about how much power they'd give their cabinets. Neither achieved his goal. "I don't want a government of yes-men," declared Nixon. "[I want] a cabinet made up of the ablest men in America." But within five years he had replaced them all, after requesting them to resign en masse. For counsel, Nixon turned instead to White House staffers H. R. Haldeman and John Erlichman. Relying on the White House staff instead of the cabinet is a route followed by most recent presidents. The staffers, after all, are people whom the president has known for many years and who have only one allegiance: to the Oval Office.

Tension between White House staffers and cabinet members is a given in every administration. Over the past couple of decades, presidents have tried alternatives to the traditional cabinet system in an effort to make the best use of both groups. One option: task forces that combine the talents of White House staffers and cabinet members. Kennedy used such a task force to handle the Cuban Missile Crisis. Nixon attempted to set up a "supercabinet" composed of four ultrapowerful members, but Congress wouldn't go along. Nixon then decided to name four cabinet members presidential counselors, so that they were combination staffers and cabinet members.

Although some political observers claim that the cabinet can never be a useful resource for the president, no one seriously considers disbanding it. Meanwhile, the mix-and-match of White House staffers and cabinet members will continue to provide us with an endless supply of task forces.

The chart below lists the fourteen departments of the U.S. government whose secretaries make up the cabinet, and the number of people each department employs.

Department	*Number of Employees*
AGRICULTURE	119,558
COMMERCE	37,642
DEFENSE	879,651**
EDUCATION	4,813
ENERGY	19,899
HEALTH AND HUMAN SERVICES	128,244
HOUSING AND URBAN DEVELOPMENT	13,218
INTERIOR	80,704
JUSTICE	97,910
LABOR	16,732
STATE	25,596
TRANSPORTATION	64,896
TREASURY	156,373
VETERANS AFFAIRS	262,432

Figures are current as of September 1994.

Civilian employees only—does not include the armed forces.

WHAT IS PORK-BARREL LEGISLATION?

Legislators are supposed to represent their constituents. So why, when a senator tries to garner government funding for his district, are his efforts sneered at as "pork"?

Pork is the cheapest meat you can buy. The *pork* in pork barrel refers to tidbits of meat (money) floating among the rest of a piece of legislation—tidbits that serve no purpose other than to line the pockets of constituents. It's a cheap way of getting votes; not cheap in the sense of inexpensive, but cheap in that it disregards the best interests of all citizens to "buy off" the votes of a few.

But what differentiates legitimate expenses from pork? That can be quite subjective. In 1991 Ralph Kinney Bennett outlined in *Reader's Digest* some of the bills that he considered pork barrel. Among them:

* $1 million to determine why people don't use bicycles or walking as a means of transportation
* $94,000 to study apple quality
* $37,000 to study management techniques for handling animal manure
* $80,000 to research how the floss from milkweed pods could replace goose down in bedding
* $3 million for neighborhood economic improvement in New Orleans

Bennett's examples are thought-provoking. Studying manure does seem to be a waste of taxpayers' money, but who is to say why $3 million *shouldn't* go to New Orleans, a city beaten down by years of recession? The Big Easy has the highest per-capita murder rate in the country, so boosting the economy (and perhaps pushing down the crime rate) probably feels more like a lifesaver than a luxury to the people living there. To residents of Memphis, however, it may seem like pure pork.

And so it goes. For every chunk of pork, there's a rationale. Sometimes the pork is a flagrant abuse of public moneys, such as when funding is granted to maintain obsolete defense programs that not even the Pentagon supports. (The rationale: It saves jobs.) Other times the issue is more complex, as in the case of the superconducting supercollider. Its budget was astronomical, but its goal was glorious: to re-create the conditions of the universe when it was $\frac{1}{100}$ quadrillionth of a second old, and to place America at the cutting edge of high-energy physics. Support for the superconductor fizzled when estimates for its construction soared to $13 billion. Congress abandoned the project in 1993, after spending $2 billion on it and building ten miles of underground tunnels in Texas. Not surprisingly, Texans who had held key positions in Washington when the Texas site was approved in 1988 had, by 1993, lost much of their political clout.

The problem isn't just that members of Congress are constantly pushing pork for their districts. It's the *way* the pork gets slipped through the legislative process: tacked on to important (unrelated) legislation at the last minute, agreed upon in meetings held behind closed doors, added to a bill hours before Congress is about to attend the last session of the season.

The only cure, say many citizens and politicians, is a line-item veto that would allow the president to "trim the pork" out of bills when they cross his desk. As things currently stand, a president must either sign or veto a bill in its entirety. In November 1994 Republicans took control of both houses of Congress, promising to make the line-item veto one of their priorities. But Republicans have grown just as addicted to pork as Democrats, so it will be interesting to see who's really willing to forgo the bacon.

WHAT IS A POCKET VETO?

If a president doesn't like a bill and believes that a presidential veto would be overruled, he can invalidate it another way: by resorting to the pocket veto. The bill must be passed by Congress less than ten days before its adjournment for the ploy to work, in which case the president simply withholds his signature. The tactic used to be called the silent, or negative, veto. The president figuratively puts the bill in his pocket and forgets about it until Congress goes home. The pocket veto allows the president to squelch a bill without giving any reason, and it's raised the ire of many a politician. In 1848 the *Ohio State Journal* referred to the technique as "the 'pocket' veto, that contrivance of tyranny to crush with inevitable death its object."

CAN THE PRESIDENT DECLARE WAR WITHOUT CONGRESS'S APPROVAL?

In theory, no. The War Powers Resolution of 1973 specifically limits the president's power to send troops "into hostilities or into situations where imminent involvement in hostilities is clearly indicated by the circumstances." A president may unilaterally order troops to respond to an attack on the United States, but in all other cases he must report to Congress within forty-eight hours if he has dispatched troops. Once a president does declare a war, a sixty-day mandatory withdrawal deadline is automatically set, unless Congress approves the action.

It sounds good, but in fact U.S. troops have seen plenty of action since 1973—in places like Grenada, Tripoli, and the Persian Gulf. The United States has been actively involved in foreign military affairs about two hundred times since the Constitution was signed, yet technically it has declared war just five times. The War Powers Resolution is only the latest compromise in a long-running dispute between Congress and the presidency over who has the power to declare war.

It was a thorny issue right from the beginning, when the framers of the Constitution argued about whether the legislature should have the right to *make* war or to *declare* it. If they only had the power to declare war, that would leave in the president's hands the power to make it—that is, to repel an attack against U.S. territory. Both Washington and Madison deferred to Congress before getting into a conflict. But our third president, Thomas Jefferson, set the tone for most of the chief executives thereafter.

Jefferson, who had been a strong advocate of congressional approval before he took office, became more independent-minded once he was in the White House. In 1803 France presented him with an extraordinary opportunity: to purchase the Louisiana Territory, from the Mississippi River to the Rocky Mountains, for $15 million. France's offer was completely unexpected, and Jefferson agreed to it knowing that he had "stretched the Constitution till it cracked." This purchase would in one fell swoop double the size of the United States. If any action warranted review by Congress, this was it. But Jefferson insisted that "to lose our country by a scrupulous adherence to written law, would be to lose the law itself, with life, liberty, property, and all who are enjoying them with us; thus absurdly sacrificing the end to the means." This chain of reasoning, referred to as the "higher law" doctrine, has been used ever since to rationalize acts taken by individuals who should have consulted Congress first.

On the whole, chief executives have had fairly good luck in pushing their military agendas through Congress. Presidents Lincoln, Wilson, and Franklin Roosevelt smoothly deflected congressional challenges to their military plans. Truman managed to send troops to Korea without ever declaring a war there, even though the situation was hotly debated in the Senate. Truman's success laid the groundwork for subsequent "interventions," most notably in Vietnam.

In 1973, after the United States already had pulled out of Vietnam, Congress finally roused itself and passed the War Powers Act. Presidents since that time have (sometimes grudgingly) told Congress about their military plans. The fall of the Soviet Union—the evaporation of America's biggest enemy—has made many Americans leery of any kind of war. What is worth fighting for, now that the democratic way of life is no longer threatened by communism? This wariness will most likely result in the War Powers Act being tested more than ever before.

Musing over the struggle between Congress and the executive branch, writer William Safire concluded that "the tension never lets up; that's the way it is supposed to be. The strength of the system is that no center of power exclusively controls the power to decide when and if we get into war, how long we stay in it, and when and how we get out of it."

What does the Supreme Court decide?

The prime function of the Supreme Court is to uphold the tenets of the U.S. Constitution. This is done through the Court's power of judicial review. Judicial review ensures that the decisions of the Court become the highest law of the land. The Court may review any law passed by Congress or the states and decide whether or not the law is constitutional. If it finds that a law doesn't meet the requirements of the Constitution, the law becomes void.

The concept of judicial review was not mentioned in the Constitution. It was developed in the 1803 case *Marbury* v. *Madison*—the most important decision in the history of the Court and of the nation. In it, Chief Justice John Marshall established the right of the Supreme Court to nullify congressional statutes if they were found to violate the Constitution.

The founding fathers didn't anticipate that the court would wield this much power. Alexander Hamilton thought the federal judiciary would be the weakest branch of government because it didn't control either money or arms. But judicial review enabled the courts to have the last word. Writing for the *New York Times Magazine,* Laurence H. Tribe explained why the Court was so well suited for this responsibility: "The very purpose of a Constitution is to place certain principles, both of individual liberty and of government structure, beyond the reach of contemporary majorities—and of those accountable to them." Both Congress and the president are accountable to political forces. Because Supreme Court justices are appointed for life, they can commit themselves to upholding the Constitution's letter and spirit without fear of losing their jobs. Certainly the different justices' political philosophies tend to reflect those of the presidents who appointed them. But time has shown that, once on the bench, most justices develop an independent style. More than a few presidents have been disappointed by the decisions of "their" justices.

The nine justices receive about 5,000 cases a year and write opinions on 150 to 160 of them. There are three possible routes by which a case can get to the Supreme Court. A lower court may request an opinion on a particular point of law. This is called *certification.* Or a case may reach the Court through the *right of appeal,* if a litigant is unsatisfied with the decision of a lower court and that decision falls into one of eight specific categories. In some cases, the Supreme Court can reject an appeal.

The great majority of cases—90 percent of them—come to the Court on a *writ of certiorari.* Whereas people have the right to appeal, certiorari is not a right but simply an option open to people unhappy with a lower court's decision. In practical terms this means that the Court can refuse to hear any of these cases. The Court accepts about 10 to 15 percent of the annual certiorari petitions.

How does the Court choose which cases to try? Each justice must review the petitions brought before him or her (they all have clerks to help them with this mammoth task). If four or more justices agree to take a case, it is placed on the docket. If a case is rejected, the decision of the lower court stands. Although this rejection isn't supposed to be a tacit approval of the lower court's ruling, the result is usually the same as if it were.

WHAT IS THE BILL OF RIGHTS?

The Bill of Rights is the first ten amendments in the U.S. Constitution. These brief passages, totaling a little over five hundred words, form the foundation of our democracy and spell out the basic individual rights Americans are guaranteed. When people speak of "Constitutional rights," they are primarily speaking of those rights protected by the first ten amendments. The Bill of Rights is the fundamental law of the land. If statutes and other governmental acts are found to be in conflict with the Bill of Rights, they may be nullified on the grounds that they are unconstitutional.

THE FIRST TEN AMENDMENTS TO THE U.S. CONSTITUTION

THE 1ST AMENDMENT. Congress shall make no law respecting an establishment of religion, or prohibiting the free exercise thereof; or abridging the freedom of speech, or of the press; or the right of the people peaceably to assemble, and to petition the Government for a redress of grievances.

THE 2ND AMENDMENT. A well regulated Militia, being necessary to the security of a free State, the right of the people to keep and bear Arms, shall not be infringed.

THE 3RD AMENDMENT. No Soldier shall, in time of peace be quartered in any house, without the consent of the Owner, nor in time of war, but in a manner to be prescribed by law.

THE 4TH AMENDMENT. The right of the people to be secure in their persons, houses, papers, and effects, against unreasonable searches and seizures, shall not be violated, and no Warrants shall issue, but upon probable cause, supported by Oath or affirmation, and particularly describing the place to be searched, and the person or things to be seized.

THE 5TH AMENDMENT. No person shall be held to answer for a capital, or otherwise infamous crime, unless on a presentment or indictment of a Grand Jury, except in cases arising in the land or naval forces, or in the Militia, when in actual service in time of War or public danger; nor shall any person be subject for the same offence to be twice put in jeopardy of life or limb, nor shall be compelled in any criminal case to be a witness against himself, nor be deprived of life, liberty, or property, without due process of law; nor shall private property be taken for public use, without just compensation.

THE 6TH AMENDMENT. In all criminal prosecutions, the accused shall enjoy the right to a speedy and public trial, by an impartial jury of the State and district wherein the crime shall have been committed; which district shall have been previously ascertained by law, and to be informed of the nature and cause of the accusation; to be confronted with the witnesses against him; to have compulsory process for obtaining witnesses in his favor, and to have the Assistance of Counsel for his defence.

THE 7TH AMENDMENT. In suits of common law, where the value in controversy shall exceed twenty dollars, the right of trial by jury shall be preserved, and no fact tried by a jury, shall be otherwise re-examined in any Court of the United States, than according to the rules of common law.

THE 8TH AMENDMENT. Excessive bail shall not be required, nor excessive fines imposed, nor cruel and unusual punishments inflicted.

THE 9TH AMENDMENT. The enumeration in the Constitution, of certain rights shall not be construed to deny or disparage others retained by the people.

THE 10TH AMENDMENT. The powers not delegated to the United States by the Constitution, nor prohibited by it to the States, are reserved to the States respectively, or to the people.

Psychobabble

✳   ✳   ✳

WHAT ARE ID, EGO, AND SUPEREGO?

The terms *id, ego,* and *superego* describe the three parts of
the human psychological structure. They come to us directly
from Sigmund Freud, but *ego* has taken on a negative sheen
the father of psychoanalysis never intended. According to
Freud, the id is the unconscious mind, the ego is the part of
the psyche that connects with and adapts to the outside world
(our conscious self), and the superego plays the role of our
conscience, or what some would call our "higher self." As
the lingo of psychology has permeated our language, *ego* has
become synonymous with an inflated sense of self. People go
on "ego trips" or have "huge egos." Id and superego, meanwhile, have faded from the general public's awareness.

WHAT IS HYSTERIA?

Although Freud did not originate the concept, hysteria was
the cornerstone of his theory of psychopathology. It was used
to describe a wide range of symptoms, and eventually that
range became so broad that the term itself was dropped from
the American Psychiatric Association's diagnostic listings.

The word *hysterical* comes from the Greek word for nervous disorders of the uterus (*hysterectomy* comes from the same roots). Freud's theories were based on his studies of women who behaved in ways he labeled hysterical. The pattern went as follows: An event would cause the patient to develop an odd physical symptom, such as paralysis, blindness, seizures, or any number of things. Freud declared that the patient achieved two psychological gains from the hysterical symptom. First, she avoided dealing with the event that triggered the symptom; second, she got to bask in the attention and support of her family and friends. This type of female hysteria was common around the turn of the century—or at least it was commonly diagnosed—but has faded from the modern scene.

Since Freud's definition of hysteria quickly expanded to include everything from psychosomatic pain to sleepwalking to amnesia, it inevitably became less and less useful as a descriptive term. Hysterical neuroses are now divided into two types, conversion and dissociative, each of which includes a number of specific mental ailments.

None of the above uses of the word *hysteria* comes very close to its current popular use, as in, "When he heard about the parking ticket he got hysterical." That implies an overly excitable soul who frequently indulges in loud, theatrical scenes. There's a name for this "Drama Queen" syndrome, too: histrionic personality disorder.

WHAT IS SUBLIMATION?

According to Freud, sublimation keeps us civilized. If we didn't sublimate some of our instincts, we'd end up in all kinds of trouble—sleeping with our mother, punching the waitress who threatens to remove the hamburger before we're finished—in short, doing exactly as the animal within us desires. The difference between sublimation and self-control is that sublimation occurs on the unconscious level. It is the prime way in which we rechannel urges that would cause us severe shame or guilt.

Sublimation is an unconscious process of substituting acceptable behavior for that which is unacceptable. It begins early in life. For example, when a toddler first learns that he can't draw on the walls he may sublimate that desire and instead draw on a pad of paper. That way he's achieved partial satisfaction by redirecting the initial urge. As the child grows up, he learns to rechannel more and more behavior this way so he can exist comfortably in society.

How much of our behavior can we chalk up to sublimation? There's a lot of debate about that. Some theorists insist that all our pursuits result from sublimated sex drives, aggression, voyeurism, and so forth. That paints a narrow picture of human nature, for while it's easy to see how aggression might be sublimated on a football field, it's less convincing to argue that research biologists are merely sublimating their voyeuristic instincts. The more complex a pursuit, especially in the areas of art and science, the less willing people are to view it as the result of redirected primitive urges.

WHAT DOES ANAL RETENTIVE MEAN?

Here's a term that is thrown around with reckless abandon. It's nearly always used to describe someone who is obsessively neat. In psychology texts the anal retentive character is defined as someone who is stingy, obstinate, and meticulous. But what does any of that have to do with the rectum?

A quick glimpse at Freud's reasoning clears up the mystery. Freud believed that between the ages of two and three a child's libido (urge for physical pleasure) is focused on defecation. The child's fascination is compounded by his diaper-weary parents' attempts to potty-train him. There are two elements to toilet training: holding it in (retention) and letting it out (expulsion). Some children get pleasure out of expulsion. They, according to Freud, will become ambitious, conceited, and generous. The ambition and conceit are due to a "job-well-done" feeling, that proud glow of satisfaction that comes with a successful bowel movement. The generosity? That's associated with the child's willingness to "give" of himself when asked.

Then there is the other sort of child, the youngster who wants to retain his feces. Freud's theory holds that this child is likely to develop into a person who is orderly, frugal, and obstinate—the "anal triad" that makes up the anal retentive character. As an adult, anal retentiveness is played out in an unwillingness to part with money, just as the child is unwilling to part with his feces. The orderliness is a response to his mother's demands to be clean. But the child also is rebelling against Mother's demand to "give up" his feces. Herein lie the roots of his obstinacy.

Now the good news: None of this is taken seriously anymore, at least insofar as creating an "anal" personality. The *International Dictionary of Psychology* puts it this way: "There is no evidence that the traits ascribed [to the anal retentive character] do in fact originate in the anal stage."

WHAT IS AN OEDIPUS COMPLEX?

Sigmund Freud developed the Oedipus complex and lay great store in it; it's one of the most important components of his theory of personality development. People usually think of the Oedipus complex as a boy/mother issue, but it applies to girls as well. Sometimes the girl's Oedipus complex is called an Electra complex, but this label never really caught on.

Although mainstream psychology owes a huge debt to many of Freud's theories, the Oedipus complex has not aged well. In fact, much of the outcry against Freudian psychology was in response to the Oedipus complex. A central theme of the complex is penis envy, a concept that has very few fans in today's psychiatric community. Modern psychologists are quick to note that Freud's own family, which consisted of a warm, loving mother and an aloof father, possibly influenced his perceptions of family dynamics enough to sully his objectivity when he developed the Oedipus complex theory. Having said all that, it's still fascinating to take a walk through Oedipal territory, especially when you consider that for years these concepts were accepted unblinkingly by millions.

The Oedipus complex has to do with the way children identify with their parents. The complex gets its name from Oedipus, the legendary Greek king who unwittingly killed his father and later married his mother. The complex is different for boys and girls, but since much of it revolves around the penis, let's look at the boys' version first.

Freud believed that a young boy has two sets of feelings toward his parents. He loves his mother and is jealous of his father; but at the same time he loves his father and is jealous of his mother. In most boys the first set of feelings—longing for the mother and jealous rage toward the father—dominates. When the boy is two or three years old, he begins to get sexual feelings; touching his penis feels good, and he becomes all the more aware of its existence. He's proud of his male organ and wants to impress Mom with it. At about the same time, he begins to see Dad as a rival, and he's driven by a strong desire to get rid of his father so he can have Mother all to himself.

On some level, Freud postulates, the boy realizes that his desire to eliminate Dad could cost him his father's love and protection. The instinct to secure the father's love is the strongest one the child has—it's an instinct for survival. And the boy has noticed another thing: Some children don't have penises. These unlucky offspring—girls—must have lost their penises somehow, the boy assumes. Maybe Dad punished the girl by castrating her. Maybe Dad will do the same to the boy if he doesn't stop wishing his father were gone. The conflict is intense and terrifying, and the boy usually resolves it by abandoning his conscious oedipal desires. When he's five or six, he begins to identify with his father, seeking to become like him rather than to get rid of him. The boy understands that he must respect his father's special place in the family and special relationship with his mother. Through all of this, the boy learns how to defer to authority. These lessons are incorporated into the part of the boy's personality Freud dubbed the **superego**.

The boy's oedipal experience is frightening, so much so that his conscious mind completely represses it when he is an adult. But when a man is drawn to a woman who is a lot like his mother, Freud believed that it is because his oedipal urges are seeping though his personality.

How do little girls fit in? They, too, have dual sets of feelings about both parents: Girls are closely bonded with their mother in infancy and are jealous of their father, while at the same time feeling love for their father and jealousy toward their mother. Then, at age two or three, a baby girl notices that she does *not* have a penis. According to Freud, this discovery brings on powerful feelings of inferiority and jealousy (the infamous penis envy). The girl becomes very attached to her dad, who has the longed-for appendage, and enraged at her mother, who not only shares her pitiful penisless condition but also is a rival for Dad's attention.

Because the girl already is "castrated," she doesn't fear

castration. She can remain oedipal—that is, attached to her father and hostile toward her mother—for a long time. Without the threat of castration to force her to get with the program (respect her mother's higher authority in the family order, keep her illicit desires under wraps, and so forth), her superego develops at a slower rate, and so ultimately is weaker than the boy's superego. The girl's weak superego makes her more vulnerable to neurosis. In short, the girl's lack of a penis prevents her from fully developing some elements of her personality that are essential to a healthy adult, making her more psychologically fragile than a man.

The penis-envy concept greatly irked generations of women who insisted they *never* envied those particular few inches of flesh. Today, the Oedipus complex is mostly viewed as the interesting but ultimately wrongheaded invention of a brilliant man.

What is a nervous breakdown?

This is a layperson's term that doesn't have a true diagnostic definition. It usually refers to a sudden neurotic or psychotic disturbance that incapacitates a person, often landing the victim in a hospital. Sometimes *nervous breakdown* is simply defined as "the inability to function due to a mental disorder"; other sources are careful to point out that nervous breakdown can mean any kind of mental disruption *short* of psychosis.

Is subconscious the same as unconscious?

"In popular psychoanalysis, the unconscious and the subconscious are thoroughly confused," says *A Comprehensive Dictionary of Psychological and Psychoanalytical Terms*. No wonder, then, that the layperson is also confused about these two layers of consciousness, which are indeed different from each other.

The *unconscious* is a term for the thought process in which beliefs, sensations, and desires are not organized into conscious perceptions. There is no self-awareness of these unconscious thoughts; the person doesn't even realize the process is going on. Unconscious thoughts are generally the result of experiences a person cannot accept on the conscious level. Instead, he or she distorts or denies the experience or represses it entirely.

The concept of an unconscious mind has existed for thousands of years. Plato believed that the unconscious was the fertile soil in which dreams, intuition, and memory dwelt, while mystics from ancient times through Jung believed that the unconscious was our portal to other spiritual planes. In his research into **hysteria** (see page 75), Freud studied the unconscious mind and concluded that there were three ways to access it: hypnosis, free association, and the interpretation of dreams. His hypothesis, and the seed from which sprang the study of psychology, is that our conscious mental processes as well as our daily behavior are partly driven by memories, desires, and associations that lie unrecognized in our unconscious mind.

Subconscious thoughts lie much closer to the surface of the conscious mind. They have not necessarily been repressed but have gone unnoticed. Subconscious thoughts linger at the edge of consciousness but can be brought to the surface relatively easily. The term *subconscious* is also used as a synonym for *preconscious*. In Freud's view, preconscious thoughts were "latent" material that could be voluntarily recalled under certain conditions, the same way a person's knowledge of French may go unused until he or she visits France.

How do subliminal messages work?

DOGSINATAS. Did an image of Satan just flash through your brain? If not, you've proven again what researchers have insisted for more than one hundred years: Subliminal messages don't work. (Dogsinatas is "Satan is god" spelled backward—the type of subliminal message some people claim is worked into the soundtracks of rock albums.)

Subliminal messages are images, sounds, or any other kind of stimuli presented at a level too low or too scrambled to be consciously perceived. In the United States the popular furor over subliminal messages began in a movie theater in the late 1950s. Advertising expert James Vicary revealed that he had secretly flashed two messages, EAT POPCORN and DRINK COCA-COLA, on a movie screen every five seconds during the presentation of a film. The messages were flashed for only ⅓₀₀₀th of a second, too briefly to be consciously registered by the human eye. But Vicary reported that theater patrons purchased 57 percent more popcorn and 18 percent more Coke than did patrons at another, unspecified screening.

Public outcry was fast and furious and led to extensive research. Again and again studies set out to answer the two salient questions about subliminal messages: Could humans perceive them at all? If they did perceive them on an unconscious level, could the messages compel people to act against their will? The second question was what had everyone so worried, for obvious reasons: If the answer was yes, mind control would be terrifyingly easy. But as the results of the studies came in, it became clear that subliminal messages were incapable of influencing anyone. The power of suggestion, it turned out, was a much more potent force.

Take the study run by the Canadian Broadcast Corporation in 1958 in an attempt to replicate the Vicary findings. The CBC flashed the words PHONE NOW 352 times during a popular television show. Nobody called the station. Telephone usage didn't go up during that period. The station later asked the viewing public to send in letters guessing what the message had been. Out of 500 guesses, not one was correct. However, aware of the Vicary study, nearly 250 people claimed they had been hungry or thirsty during the show.

Yet for all the evidence to the contrary, the concept of subliminal messages continues to appeal to people. Reports surface regularly claiming that sexual images are inserted into print advertising. They may be. But there is no evidence that these images prompt readers to do anything.

In the mid 1980s a new wave of concern rose over so-called "backward messages" that rock bands supposedly were inserting into their recordings to lure hapless teens into the dark realms of Satan. An extensive study was conducted in Canada to test these claims. The results were conclusive, as the *Encyclopedia of Psychology* reports:

> Backward messages are ineffective in altering behavior. . . . subjects could not (1) discriminate a backward question from a backward statement; (2) tell if two backward messages had the same or different meaning; (3) distinguish nonsense from meaningful backward messages; and (4) distinguish between backward nursery rhymes, Christian, satanic, pornographic, or advertising messages.

The news that subliminal messages are powerless to influence us (or even to register correctly in our subconsciousness) should have been a relief to everyone. Everyone, that is, except the producers and consumers of subliminal self-help audiotapes, which remain popular despite all the scientific research. There have been nine independent studies done on the tapes, all of which found that the manufacturers' claims were basically bogus.

The issue of subliminal recorded messages climaxed in 1990 when Judge Jerry Carr Whitehead ruled in favor of the rock band Judas Priest and their label, CBS Records. Judas Priest had been charged with inserting a subliminal message into one of their songs, a message that allegedly encouraged two teenagers to kill themselves. (The message: "Do it.") Judge Whitehead ruled that there simply was no scientific evidence to support the claim that a subliminal message precipitated the suicides.

WHAT'S THE DIFFERENCE BETWEEN A SOCIOPATH AND A PSYCHOPATH?

None. *Sociopath* and *psychopath* are just two of the labels that have been used to describe what is currently called *antisocial personality disorder*. The condition has mystified psychologists and the general population ever since it was first described, under the term *moral insanity,* back in 1835.

Moral insanity, though it is no longer used, does get to the essence of the affliction. The man who thought up the term defined the problem this way: "The moral or active principles of the mind are strangely perverted or depraved . . . the individual is found to be incapable, not of talking or reasoning upon any subject proposed to him but of conducting himself with decency and propriety in the business of life."

The term *psychopathic inferiority* evolved about fifty years later, when psychologists were playing with the idea that this lack of moral sense might be a congenital deficit akin to mental retardation. (This concept was soon discarded.) In 1930 a new name was introduced: *sociopath*. This label put the emphasis on the arena in which the individual most visibly failed, namely, society. Sociopaths didn't experience guilt or remorse. They lied regularly and, eerily, they had no insight as to why their behavior was unacceptable. The American Psychiatric Association settled on the label *sociopathic personality pattern* for the illness, and later changed it again to *antisocial personality disorder. Psychopath* was rejected because the word had become a dumping ground for any unclassifiable type of nuttiness. But though the label *psychopath* has not been officially sanctioned for more than twenty-five years, it is still widely used both in the media and among psychiatric professionals.

What, exactly, is this creature? In *The Mask of Sanity,* first published in 1955 and updated in 1982, Hervey Cleckly attempts to pin down the psychopath. He writes: "In all the orthodox psychoses . . . there is a more or less obvious alteration of reasoning processes or of some other demonstrable personality feature. In the psychopath this is not seen. The observer is confronted with a convincing mask of sanity." This mask is not just two-dimensional—it is "a solid and substantial structural image of the sane and rational personality." And Cleckly offers this chilling conclusion:

We are dealing here not with a complete man at all but with something that suggests a subtly constructed reflex machine that can mimic the human personality perfectly. . . . So perfect is this reproduction of a whole and normal man that no one who examines a psychopath in a clinical setting can point out in scientific or objective terms why, or how, he is not real. And yet we eventually come to know or feel we know that reality, in the sense of full, healthy experiencing of life, is not here.

WHAT'S THE DIFFERENCE BETWEEN AN INNER CHILD, A WOUNDED CHILD, AND AN ADULT CHILD?

In the 1980s pop psychology seemed to be everywhere: on talk shows, on news shows, and especially in bookstores, where literature sections shrunk and self-help sections expanded with the unstoppable energy of the Blob. The inner child's sticky paw prints were all over the scene of the crime. Who is this inner kid?

Though it became hugely popular only in the mid-1980s, the concept of the inner child entered the psychiatric scene more than thirty years ago. It was largely the brainchild of Carl Jung, who wrote:

> In every adult there lurks a child—an eternal child, something that is always becoming, is never completed, and calls for unceasing care, attention, and education. That is the part of the human personality which wants to develop and become whole.

The inner child is the part of us that some would call the soul; it is the essence of our selves. The inner child is innocent and curious, truthful and intuitive, spontaneous and guileless.

It goes without saying that very few of us manage to grow to adulthood with an unsullied inner child. Merely by growing up, we inevitably lose our innocence; we do what we must to survive. For most people childhood itself is fraught with potential disaster and humiliation, if not on the playground then at the hands of our imperfect parents and siblings. Some people, though, have truly awful childhoods. These people are said to have a "wounded" inner child.

Where the terms get confusing is when the *adult child* comes into the picture. *Adult child* is shorthand for "Adult Child of an Alcoholic." The Adult Children of Alcoholics

(ACA) movement is a spin-off of Alcoholics Anonymous, the granddaddy of all twelve-step recovery programs. An "ACA" refers specifically to someone who grew up in a family where one or both parents were alcoholics. The ACA program relies heavily on the concept of the inner child. By recognizing and validating traumatic childhood experiences, the adult child can begin to understand what drives some of his or her behavior, and through understanding it, "heal" the wounded inner child.

The inner-child concept has always been controversial. The most frequent complaint is that the criteria for having a wounded inner child seem a little lax. Some of the movement's leaders insist that nearly everyone is wounded, damaged by shame and guilt. But one aspect of the inner-child movement has been unquestionably positive. This is the realization that child abusers most likely were abused themselves. Because of their "damaged inner child," they do not understand the proper way to parent, and they in turn abuse their own children. Though this "chain of abuse" was recognized long before the inner-child phenomenon occurred, the movement has helped raise consciousness on child abuse and ways to prevent it.

What is acting out? Is there such a thing as acting in?

The term *acting out* is often applied to children, a sort of psychologically correct way to say "throwing a tantrum": "Bobby was really acting out in the supermarket today." Acting out, from a diagnostic point of view, is a little more complicated. *The Encyclopedia of Psychoanalysis* defines it as a "discharge of infantile wishes that the patient does not usually consciously connect·with repressed wishes." When a patient acts out, he is responding to a present situation in a way that is determined by older, repressed drives. Instead of recognizing and trying to understand the feelings that motivate him, the patient uses an unrelated behavior to release the tension these feelings cause. It can be impulsive, uncontrolled behavior, such as shouting at your child when you're really stewing over a problem at work, or more subtle, such as responding to your car's high repair bills by neglecting to wash the car. Interestingly, the *International Dictionary of Psychology* declares that *acting out* "can be defined more succinctly as any behavior on the part of the patient of which the therapist disapproves."

What about *acting in*? Acting in is acting out that occurs during the analytic session itself. For instance, if the analyst asks you a touchy question and you respond by commenting on how lovely her dress is, you're acting in. It's an obscure term, but it does show up in some of the literature.

WHAT IS ALIENATION?

The concept originated in the nineteenth century with Friedrich Hegel, Ludwig Feuerbach, and most important, Karl Marx. Some historians trace the idea back as far as the Old Testament and Plato, but the modern sense of the term—being estranged from society or ourselves—comes from Marx.

Although most theories that are used in psychology overlap with those of sociology, philosophy, and other disciplines, this is especially true of alienation. To Marx it was a philosophical question. In *Economic and Philosophical Manuscripts*, written in 1844, Marx explained his theory of alienation: Man alienates himself from the product of his own actions, so those products become outside objects that control him. Examples: When man imagines there to be a "higher being" (God) outside himself, he is alienating himself from his own spiritual essence. Instead he becomes a slave to a God that is separate from himself. When man deals in capital, he alienates himself from the actual fruit of his labor. When man cedes control of his destiny to governments, he is alienating the product of his social activity. Thus almost anything humans believe in or do results in self-alienation. Combined, these different types of alienation add up to the alienation of humans from their humanness.

In the socialist state, Marx believed, men and women would be the masters of their own will and destiny, and alienation would disappear. But alienation as a concept apart from socialist doctrine didn't catch on until the *Manuscripts* were published in 1932, nearly a century after Marx wrote them. Suddenly alienation captured the popular imagination. From the late 1940s until now, the concept has been a lightning rod for discussion in nearly every field of social science.

One continuing chicken-and-egg argument asks, Is a person who can't adjust to society alienated, or is today's "sick society" itself alienated, rendering the person who can't adjust to it healthy by comparison? Among those who consider alienation a purely psychological phenomenon, there are those who believe it's a way of feeling, and those who insist it's also a way of behaving. Some think it's a type of pathology, others believe that it's not. Some people argue that the concept of alienation belongs not in the field of psychology but in those of economics, politics, or sociology. Some declare that alienation is a strictly philosophical concept. In short, nearly every field has claimed and disclaimed alienation. People are obsessed with alienation and how to overcome it.

Socialists have always believed that their form of government would create the right atmosphere to "de-alienate" the individual. History isn't bearing this out. For the rest of us, there doesn't appear to be any sign of relief on the horizon. In 1960 Murray Levin observed that "the essential characteristic of the alienated man is his belief that he is not able to fulfill what he believes is his rightful role in society." An observer in the mid-1990s would instantly add that many men and women don't even know what the role should be, much less how to fulfill it.

IS EVERYONE DESTINED TO HAVE AN IDENTITY CRISIS?

Erik Erikson, who originated the concept of the identity crisis, believed that the ego goes through eight stages of development, each characterized by a crisis. The most profound of these happens in adolescence. A person's identity evolves as he rebalances all previous self-images in light of what he thinks the future will be. Adolescents, making the profound shift out of childhood, have a tremendous amount of rebalancing to do and are especially unnerved by their future—the uncharted territory of adulthood. Traditional cultures had puberty rituals to help teenagers ford these psychological rapids. Our culture has few such rituals.

Other than teenagers, who is most vulnerable to identity crises? Immigrants, veterans, welfare recipients who feel the sting of society's disapproval . . . and then there are the stages of life after adolescence at which the sense of identity is especially precarious for everyone. Studies in the late 1970s warned that you're treading treacherous ground from the teen years until about age thirty-three, as you move through college to young adulthood, get married, perhaps get divorced, and continue to reevaluate your career and life. From thirty-three to forty you may get a breather, but somewhere between forty and forty-five, it's midlife crisis time. If you don't have another identity crisis when you retire, you'll probably have one as you near death.

Calling every one of these transitional periods a crisis may be needlessly alarming. In 1976 Gail Sheehy coined the term *passages* for the same transitions. A passage sounds reassuringly inevitable, whereas a crisis sounds like a car wreck that healthy (and lucky) people can avoid. Whether someone views a transition as a crisis or a passage or a challenge may also depend on the way the media is presenting the concept that week.

At the height of the cultural revolution in 1968 Erikson himself wondered, "Would some of our youth act so openly confused and confusing if they did not know they were supposed to have an identity crisis?"

WHAT IS AN ARCHETYPE?

The word is derived from the Greek, *arche* ("primal") and *typos* ("figure" or "pattern"). It's been used since the time of Plato, but Carl Jung redefined it for the twentieth century and the age of psychoanalysis.

Jung was a follower of Freud in the early 1900s, but in about 1912 they parted ways over Jung's theories of the collective unconscious and archetypes ("Jung is crazy," Freud wrote to a friend). Freud believed the ego is the center of the human psyche and the unconscious is a sort of holding tank for repressed urges. Jung theorized that the center of the human psyche was the self, an entity composed not only of primal drives and unique characteristics but also of a universal essence. These aspects of the psyche existed in two layers: the personal unconscious, which held the memories and effects of individual experiences in this lifetime, and the collective unconscious, which consisted of archetypes—primordial images that are inherited within the species. The archetypes have been part of human consciousness since earliest times. They aren't specific entities but "patterns," vessels to be filled in by current experience.

To Jung, archetypes were the most important aspect of the

psyche, giving form to almost everything we perceive. He compared archetypes to instincts: Instincts are a natural tendency to act a certain way, while archetypes are a natural tendency to perceive experience in a certain way.

The same archetypes have been observed in religion, folklore, and mythology of cultures throughout the world. Jung felt that the most important of these included the shadow, the animus and anima (archetypal male and female ego, respectively), the wise old man, the earth mother, the child, and the self. They usually appear in personified form, and they exist in many realms. They may be figures in dreams, or religious icons, or characters in a child's fairy tale. There are no good or bad archetypes; each can represent positive or negative qualities. Jung also identified archetypes of transformation—situations, places, and events that express universal patterns and which recur in the folklore and myths of all cultures.

WHAT DO ALL THOSE LETTERS BEHIND THERAPISTS' NAMES MEAN?

Anyone who has sought psychiatric help recently knows that there is a bewildering array of therapists offering every type of "talking cure" from traditional analysis to past-life regression. The field of psychology is still very young, and new discoveries, particularly about the biochemical components of mental illness, keep shifting the ground beneath therapists' feet. This means you have to be careful whom you hire to heal your inner child, deconstruct your neuroses, or decode your dreams.

If you go out shopping for a psychologist, the first thing you'll notice is that they have different professional designations. These are consistent throughout the United States, but licensing requirements vary dramatically from state to state. One thing that differs widely is the number of supervised internship hours the therapist must put in before going it alone. Many free or inexpensive mental health clinics employ graduate students in psychology who are filling up their internship requirements. This doesn't mean they are bad, it just means they're less experienced than licensed therapists. All licensed therapists must, at the minimum, be college graduates and either be an RN (registered nurse) or have completed a master's degree in psychology. Here are the basic categories of therapist:

✳ MFC: MASTERS IN FAMILY COUNSELING. There are various types of master's level counselors; the MFC is a very common one because of the past decade's emphasis on family dynamics. Master's of Counseling degrees require one or two years of graduate study, some clinical internship hours, and sometimes a thesis.

✳ MSW: MASTER OF SOCIAL WORK. These therapists are also called psychiatric social workers. They're usually employed in clinics and hospitals. They must complete an undergraduate degree and a master's program from an accredited school of social work.

✳ PH.D.: CLINICAL PSYCHOLOGIST. These practitioners must complete a doctoral program in psychology, including a dissertation. They're trained to evaluate behavior disorders, provide therapy, consult with other professionals, and do research. They are also trained to work closely with the rest of a patient's health-care team—doctors, MSWs, psychiatrists, and so forth.

✳ PSY.D.: DOCTOR OF PSYCHOLOGY. This degree was created for people who felt that the heavy emphasis on research required by a doctoral dissertation was irrelevant to their future work as a clinical psychologist. Psy.D. degrees emphasize clinical training and do not require a dissertation. Not all schools have APA-approved Psy.D. programs, so you won't come across this credential all that often.

✳ ABD PSYCHOLOGIST. These psychologists have met all the requirements for a Ph.D. in psychology except for writing the dissertation. The ABD stands for "All But Dissertation," and is an informal label, not a credential. There are many ABD psychologists in practice. They are paid less than psychologists with Ph.D.'s and often operate under pressure to finish the dissertation. In terms of assessing them from a client's point of view, you may want to make certain that they have completed all the clinical internship hours required for a Ph.D.

✳ M.D.: PSYCHIATRIST. These men and women are physicians who diagnose and treat mental illness. They go to medical school, complete internships, and must pass state licensing requirements to practice medicine. They then embark on a residency program, usually in a mental hospital. The professional training includes:

1. One year of hospital internship
2. Three years' residency in a hospital or agency specializing in mental disorders.
3. At least two years' additional experience—required before the doctor can be certified by the American Board of Psychiatry and Neurology.

Psychiatrists are the only practitioners who can prescribe drugs or administer electroshock therapy. Some psychiatrists are also trained in psychoanalysis.

WHAT IS NORMAL?

In order to cure psychologically "abnormal" personalities, doesn't there need to be a model for a normal personality? Until the late 1950s, the answer seemed to be no. No one had seriously tried to define *normal*; an index to Freud's *Collected Papers* listed four hundred references to neurosis and not one to health. Even the APA's *Diagnostic and Statistical Manual of Mental Disorders* is silent on the topic.

Part of the problem is that healthy people go about their business unnoticed; they aren't gathered into clinics for observation. And there is certainly less reason to observe them, since they are not disrupting society. Still, as the study of psychology blossomed in the mid-twentieth century, some therapists began to outline the parameters of an ideal "healthy" personality.

Regardless of the discipline they followed, these psychologists distinguished between *normal* and *healthy*. The concept of normality was usually equated with an absence of obviously neurotic or psychotic symptoms, the same way a person who has no physical illness is considered healthy. That wasn't adequate for the psychologists, who preferred a positive definition of mental health rather than a negative one. In other words, they wanted to pinpoint particular attributes that would add up to a healthy personality, not just to define healthy as "not sick."

But for each type of therapy, the criteria for mental health was somewhat different. The *Encyclopedia of Psychology* goes to the heart of the issue: "Theories of psychological health are often based upon the views of the individual that each tradition has. . . . Each tradition's view of the individual is a *belief system* (implicit or explicit) describing human nature. Yet up to this point, no one knows what human nature is."

The different schools of psychology are based on different philosophical beliefs about human nature. They can be broken down into four broad groups. Within each group, the concept of a healthy personality is different:

✳ HUMAN NATURE IS INNATELY EVIL OR AMORAL. This is the view held by traditional Christianity and by Freud. In the Christian view, humans must seek salvation and God. Freud believed that humans are born amoral, that they are driven by a primitive, aggressive id that seeks pleasure at any cost and is brimming with anger. In this model, there is no theory of a healthy personality; people are classified as neurotic or not so neurotic. The degree to which a person is mentally healthy is based on how well he balances the three systems of the personality—**id, ego,** and **superego**—and on how well he **sublimates** his socially unacceptable urges. Most modern psychologists find this view not only bleak but inadequate in describing mental health.

✳ HUMAN NATURE IS INNATELY GOOD. This theory suggests that humans are born with the potential and the inclination to be good, but to realize this innate goodness they must be encouraged to become self-actualized, that is, to uncover the self that society sometimes stifles. This is the basis of humanist psychology, which is practiced by most contemporary therapists. Psychological health isn't seen as a fixed point, but as a continuous, ever more autonomous movement toward "higher ground"—toward reaching individual potential and learning to cope more smoothly with life's challenges. It isn't necessary to be completely self-actualized to be healthy; 100 percent self-actualized humans are about as common as saints. Rather, it's a goal to strive for.

✳ HUMANS ARE BORN AS BLANK SLATES, NEITHER GOOD NOR EVIL, AND THEY CREATE THEMSELVES. This is an existential view that is held by behavioral psychologists, among others. The theory holds that people aren't driven by uncontrollable urges or by innate decency. Rather, they simply react to environmental stimuli. In behavioral therapy, the therapist and the patient agree to work together to modify a particular unacceptable behavior. Behaviorists believe that the individual creates him or herself; the goal is to be free to embark on this project, the self.

✳ THE HUMAN SELF IS, IN ESSENCE, "NO SELF," OR PART OF A LARGER SELF. This is a philosophical view reflected in many Eastern religions. It is included in the *Encyclopedia of Psychology*'s four groups because "insofar as religious systems represent an attempt to heal the mental and physical distress of the individual, and . . . create mental and physical well-being," they can be considered a legitimate type of psychotherapy. The Eastern religions do outline a healthy personality, the traits of which include determination, adaptability, compassion, a sense of meaning, loss of self-importance, and kindness.

Where does that leave us in terms of the original question, What is normal? First, the word *normal* isn't relevant to psychologists; they think in terms of "healthy personality." Whether or not you have a healthy personality depends on your belief system and the way that system defines healthy. But as complex as this sounds, there are therapists who've developed lists of personality traits they consider to be the mark of a healthy individual, and which can be applied pretty much across the board. While the listing of traits raises the ire of psychologists intent on studying the human personality in greater depth, lists at least provide some point of reference for the average Joe who wonders about his or her mental health in this "dysfunctional" society. Among psychologists who've studied the topic, then, there is general agreement that healthy people:

* expand their understanding of themselves throughout their life
* expand their consciousness of other people and the world around them
* grow more competent in dealing with challenges
* grow in response to threat
* develop satisfying interpersonal relationships
* create realistic and fulfilling roles for themselves in society
* exercise self-control
* accept personal responsibility
* have ideals

Healthy Curiosity

✳   ✳   ✳

WHAT ARE UV-A AND UV-B RAYS, AND WHY ARE THEY BAD?
The sun emits three kinds of ultraviolet (UV) radiation waves:
UV-A, UV-B, and UV-C. (For an explanation of *waves*, see
page 161.) UV-C waves are entirely absorbed by the ozone
layer before they reach Earth, but the other two do make it
through the atmosphere. The waves, also called rays, are in-
visible but cause much damage to human skin, in the form
of wrinkling, sagging, and skin cancer.

UV-A waves are longer than UV-B waves, and until the
early 1980s many scientists considered UV-A radiation to be
safe. Attention was focused on UV-B waves, which are
shorter and 800 to 1,000 times as potent as UV-A waves in
terms of burning the skin. UV-B rays penetrate the top layer
of skin, causing damage to DNA and thickening the epider-
mis (the outer layer). They also cause the skin to tan by trig-
gering the production of melanin, which darkens the skin in
the body's effort to protect itself from radiation. Exposure to
UV-B rays has long been known to raise the risk of skin
cancer.

What about UV-A rays? Scientists now assert that the

longer UV-A rays have properties that make them quite dangerous as well. They are more prevalent than UV-B, and they can penetrate through glass, which UV-B cannot.

Children are particularly susceptible to the effects of ultraviolet rays. The Skin Cancer Foundation warns that people get the majority of their lifetime sun dose by the age of eighteen; a single bad case of sunburn in childhood may double the chance of melanoma (skin cancer) later. Ultraviolet rays are also believed to cause cataracts and other eye problems as people get older.

How can you protect yourself against UV rays? By avoiding the sun when it's at its strongest (between 10:00 A.M. and 2:00 P.M.), wearing protective clothing and sunglasses, and by using sunscreen with the appropriate SPF rating. What's SPF? Read on.

WHAT DOES SPF STAND FOR, AND WHAT DO ALL THE NUMBERS MEAN?

SPF stands for Sun Protection Factor. The Food and Drug Administration set up standards for SPF in 1978, and now all sunblocks carry an SPF number. The number primarily applies to UV-B rays, and it represents the multiple of the amount of time you can spend in the sun without burning. This makes it an individualized rating system, which is why sunscreens don't promise, say, eight hours of protection—the rating depends on how long it takes *you* to burn. For example, if you normally burn in thirty minutes with no sunscreen, a rating of SPF 20 is supposed to protect you for ten hours ($30 \times 20 = 600$ minutes, or 10 hours). But the season, your location, and the time of day must be factored in to the equation. Midday in the Bahamas in mid-July will fry you a lot faster than 3 P.M. on Coney Island in September.

SPF numbers originally were limited to between 2 and 15, but you can now buy special sunscreens with an SPF of 50.

It's questionable, though, if all that extra SPF will do you much good. The American Academy of Dermatology advises everyone to use a minimum of SPF 15, which reduces UV-B rays by 93 percent. But SPF 30—which allows you to stay in the sun twice as long—provides only 97 percent protection from UV-B rays, just 4 percent more than SPF 15. What the higher numbers can provide is some additional protection against UV-A rays, now thought to perhaps be as potentially dangerous as UV-B.

Can you just slather on more sunscreen to get more or longer protection? No. Reapplying the sunscreen does not extend the time you have until you burn. But do put on enough sunscreen in the first place (about one ounce) and reapply it every few hours to get the full protection promised on the label. Keep in mind, too, that waterproof sunscreen isn't impervious to towels: Unless you drip dry, you'll probably wipe off the sunscreen when you dry your body. Finally, always make sure children wear plenty of sunscreen (at least SPF 15; most children's sunscreens have a higher rating). And all of you, stay out of the sun between 10:00 A.M. and 2:00 P.M.!

DOES EATING GARLIC MAKE YOU HEALTHY?

The most recent medical studies indicate that garlic can indeed protect against a whole range of diseases, if not evil spirits and vampires. Ancient Egyptian sages reported twenty-two medicinal uses for garlic, and according to folklore, garlic can do everything from healing open wounds to extending the life of those who eat it religiously. To an amazing degree, science bears this out.

The biochemistry of a garlic bulb is extremely complex. Bruising or crushing a clove sets off a stream of chemical reactions that form dozens of compounds that are credited with having medicinal effects. The way in which you cook garlic, how fresh it is, and whether you're using a processed form of the bulb such as garlic powder also affects its medicinal properties. Fresh garlic, either raw or cooked, provides the most benefits. One or two cloves a day should suffice.

What can garlic do? The list is impressive:

✳ GARLIC CAN LOWER THE RISK OF STOMACH CANCER. As Louis Pasteur discovered in 1858, garlic kills bacteria. Since then, researchers have found that garlic inhibits bacterial growth in the stomach. Some stomach bacteria convert food into nitrosamines, which are carcinogenic. So inhibiting the nitrosamines may reduce the possibility of cancer. Garlic also impedes the growth of ulcer-causing bacteria that appear to raise the risk of stomach cancer.

✳ GARLIC MAY IMPEDE OTHER CANCERS. Studies have shown that garlic can slow the growth of cancer in the colon, rectum, esophagus, breast, and skin.

✳ GARLIC MAY HELP PREVENT HEART DISEASE. Garlic appears to make blood platelets less "sticky," meaning that they are less likely to clump together and form dangerous clots. Garlic also seems to reduce atherosclerosis, or hardening of the arteries.

✳ GARLIC CAN LOWER BLOOD CHOLESTEROL. In a recent study, people who consumed the equivalent of up to a clove of garlic a day had their cholesterol drop about 9 percent, a significant amount for cholesterol.

Garlic can also be used as an antiseptic to kill fungus and some bacteria, but efforts to turn it into a drug have fizzled because it's smelly and has a short shelf life. Garlic's healing powers are at their peak when it's used in food. Can you get nearly the same benefits from garlic pills? Garlic powder pills come closest in potency to the real live clove, but you'll still smell like you've had a hearty Italian dinner. If you decide to try pills, make sure they're coated, since stomach acids destroy the healthful compounds in uncoated pills.

WHAT IS HOMEOPATHIC MEDICINE?

Founded in the 1790s, homeopathic medicine is based on the theory that symptoms of disease don't necessarily indicate an organism's collapse, but instead are the organism's adaptive reaction to infections or stress—a reaction designed to reregulate and heal the organism naturally.

The easiest way to understand this theory is to consider fevers. For many years people believed fevers must be "brought down" in order for a person to return to health. While it is true that extremely high fevers can be dangerous, it's now widely recognized that a fever is the body's way of burning out an infection—that is, of making the environment too hot for the infection to thrive.

Homeopathic medicine attempts to "steer" the body's natural, self-regulating impulses. The medicines, derived from plant, mineral, or animal substances, are prescribed for their ability to mimic symptoms. In the case of a fever, for example, belladonna might be prescribed, since it causes fever. The homeopath must be a very astute judge of both the symptoms and the patient; he or she must be able to view the symptoms in the context of the whole person. Thus each homeopathic prescription is highly individualized.

What makes homeopathy so controversial? For one thing, the minuscule amount of medicine that is typically prescribed. Homeopathic medicines are created by a method of serial dilution, in which a substance is diluted in distilled water, shaken, diluted again, shaken, and so forth. Homeopaths commonly prescribe medicines that have been diluted many, many times—so many, in fact, that according to principles of chemistry and physics no molecules of the original substance should be left in the final medicine. If that's the case, how can they work? Is there any proof that they *do* work? That they aren't simply psychological fixes whose healing power lies entirely in the patient's mind?

There have, in fact, been a number of scientific studies which have shown that homeopathic medicines have a real effect on some patients. The medicines seem to be particularly useful for treatment of arthritis, migraine headaches, allergies and hay fever, flu, respiratory infections, postoperative infections, injuries, and certain complications of childbirth.

Why they work is still a mystery, but there are a few intriguing theories. One is that the distilled water in which the medicine is diluted stores the "memory" of the substance as well as the wavelength the substance radiated (all matter radiates energy). This tiny echo of the substance may be sufficient to affect brain chemistry and therefore, disease. And if the vibrations of these submolecular particles provide just a nudge to a vibration of a similar frequency (the fever-causing vibration of belladonna to the natural fever vibration in one's body, for example), it may set up a resonance that is greater than the original vibration, thus speeding up the body's natural healing process.

There are plenty of other theories about how homeopathy works—researchers from France to Southampton University to Cal Tech have explored the phenomenon. But even though no one's come up with an absolute answer, it does seem clear that homeopathy helps many people feel better. Certainly there is little to risk by giving it a try. If it works for you, that's all the proof you'll need. (Of course, no type of medicine, homeopathic or otherwise, should be given to children without consulting a doctor.)

WHAT IS A MACROBIOTIC DIET?

The macrobiotic diet is part belief system, part strict vegan/vegetarian diet. The regimen calls for eating almost no animal products. Foods are classified as "Yin" and "Yang" depending on their "activity characteristics in the universe," says the *Encyclopedia of Food Science, Food Technology, and Nutrition.* "This Yin and Yang classification does not correspond to food grouping systems based on nutrient composition."

Like the vegan/vegetarian diet, the macrobiotic diet severely limits foods that can readily provide high-quality protein, iron, calcium, zinc, riboflavin, and vitamins B-12 and D. Dairy products, meat, and sugar are forbidden. The diet consists of cereals, soybeans, fruits, nuts and seeds, vegetables, and small portions of fish. From these, it is possible to create combinations that provide the needed nutrients, but doing so on a regular basis requires the sort of planning that only the truly dedicated will carry out.

One thing the diet is good for is staying lean, since it is nearly devoid of fats. But leanness can be dangerous for pregnant women, lactating mothers, and children. Children must get the proper nutrients and fat in order to thrive, and the macrobiotic diet often doesn't measure up. The result is youngsters who are smaller, lighter, leaner, and who grow more slowly than average kids. Sometimes they catch up in later preschool and school years. (Perhaps because they're able to avail themselves of a wider variety of food when Mom and Dad aren't monitoring the meals?)

WHAT IS THE DIFFERENCE BETWEEN GOOD CHOLESTEROL AND BAD CHOLESTEROL?

You probably don't remember the exact day you became aware of cholesterol. One moment you were a carefree kid devouring a double-dip ice cream cone, the next you were an anxious bran eater fretting over the side panels of cookie boxes. Somewhere in between—a few years after cholesterol entered the scene—you heard that there were actually two types of cholesterol. One, HDL, was good. The other, LDL, was bad. Was this great news, or simply another dose of confusing data to complicate your life? Chances are you never found out.

Here, then, is the short answer about cholesterol. Pure cholesterol is an essential element of the human body. It builds sex hormones and cell membranes, and it aids digestion. Cholesterol gets its bad rep from how it's transported through the bloodstream. *Low-density lipoproteins* (LDLs) are called "bad" cholesterol because if they are forced to carry too much cholesterol, they deposit the excess in arteries. These deposits can clog arteries, which in turn can cause heart attacks and other problems. "Good" cholesterol is carried by *high-density lipoproteins* (HDLs), which absorb excess cholesterol in the bloodstream. Not only does HDL absorb cholesterol from the blood, it may even remove built-up deposits, called plaque, from artery walls.

Scientists have long known that having too high an LDL cholesterol count is bad for you. Many now believe that having too low an HDL count could also be dangerous. What can you do to raise your good cholesterol? It's harder to raise HDL than it is to lower LDL, but luckily many of the same techniques apply: Eat foods that are low in saturated fat and get as much exercise as you can. For high-risk patients there are prescription drugs; some of the drugs that lower LDL also have been shown to raise HDL.

Don't hold your breath waiting for a "good-cholesterol pill" that will enable you to eat all the French fries you want while maintaining a 150 cholesterol count. The metabolic process by which cholesterol cycles through the body is extremely complex, and HDL's part in it is not entirely understood. For now, the rules stay the same: Eat well, stay fit, and keep reading those product labels.

WHAT IS "FULL-BLOWN AIDS"?

Full-blown AIDS is a phrase frequently used by the media, and it sounds rather inexact. But full-blown AIDS does have a precise definition: It is a case of HIV infection that meets the requirements of the Centers for Disease Control's (CDC) case definition. The CDC's requirements have changed over the years, and have often been the target of criticism. The CDC definition of AIDS is extremely important to those suffering from the disease, since their access to medication, treatment, and other benefits often depends upon their illness receiving a clinical diagnosis of "CDC AIDS."

The definition of AIDS that was used in the mid-1980s was criticized for being too rigid and for ignoring many of the physical manifestations of HIV that are seen in women. The most recent classification went into effect in 1993, and it contains expanded definitions for adolescents and adults. A copy of the definition, along with other AIDS-related material, can be ordered by calling the CDC National AIDS Information Clearinghouse at 800-458-5231.

HOW CAN SOMEONE'S HAIR TURN GRAY OVERNIGHT?

We've all heard stories about a person turning gray over the course of a few days, usually following some traumatic event.

It's true; this does happen, or at least appear to happen, but the person must have some gray hairs in the first place. Typically the dark hairs outnumber the gray ones, so that the latter go unnoticed until the event occurs.

Here's how it works. Hair follicles create hair in three phases: the growing phase, which takes two to six years; the resting phase, in which the hair rests for a few weeks; and the telogen phase, in which the hair separates from the follicle. When the follicle returns to the growing phase, the new hair pushes the old hair out. A very stressful experience can trigger an autoimmune disorder called *alopecia areata*. This disorder affects old hairs that are far along in the growing phase, causing them to fall out in a matter of days rather than months. On a head of hair with both dark and gray strands, most of the old strands will be dark. When they fall out, they leave behind a higher proportion of gray strands. Thus, it appears that the person has turned gray "overnight."

CAN YOU GET ALL THE VITAMINS YOU NEED FROM A BOWL OF CEREAL?
Technically, yes. But if the rest of your diet is unhealthy it won't do you much good.

Let's start with the RDAs—Recommended Dietary Allowances—that cereal boxes list. These are estimates, very broad estimates, of the amounts of essential nutrients a healthy person needs. RDAs are not specific targets everyone must meet. RDAs are not minimal daily requirements; they aren't *required* allowances at all. They are simply guidelines. Even if you get substantially less of a nutrient than the amount listed on the cereal box, you won't necessarily suffer from a nutritional deficiency.

In fact, unless you have a very restricted diet, you're probably getting all the vitamins and minerals you need in the food you regularly eat. Getting your vitamins this way is better than getting them in cereal (or pill) form because each type of food contains elements that maximize the body's ability to absorb the nutrients it provides. Besides, vitamins and minerals are not the only ingredients that keep a body running smoothly. Fiber, carbohydrates, protein, and other substances are also essential. Some cereals are a good source of fiber; others are a cheap thrill of artificial flavoring and sugar. But no matter how ultrafortified your cereal is, your entire diet must be balanced and relatively healthy. If it is and you can't face the morning without your Trix, go for it. It's a cereal, not a vaccination.

ARE "NATURAL" OR "ORGANIC" VITAMINS BETTER THAN SYNTHETIC VITAMINS?

No. The body absorbs both the same way, and doesn't differentiate between organic and synthetic. *Food* is better than vitamins, regardless of their source. Very few people in the United States have vitamin deficiencies, and for most of us vitamin supplements are not necessary.

WHAT CAN YOU CATCH IN A HOT TUB?

Lots of things—and don't rely on chlorine for protection, even if the smell of it nearly chokes you. In hot water it's difficult to maintain levels of chlorine gas strong enough to kill bacteria. And bacteria aplenty are simmering in most hot tubs and saunas, even ones that are rigorously maintained.

The most common bacterial infection produced in hot tubs is a red, itchy rash that can't be treated and lasts about ten days. The rash is often accompanied by a sore throat, sore eyes, chills, fever, nausea, and cramps. The organism responsible for Legionnaire's disease has been found in some whirlpools, and even relatives of the tuberculosis bacterium have been linked to hot tubs, although these are not widespread problems. Herpes infections are something of a risk: Herpes simplex virus can thrive for four and a half hours on benches and wet towels near hot tubs (although not in the tubs themselves).

How can you protect yourself? You can avoid hot tubs altogether, but for many people that's too high a price to pay. The incredible relaxation that sets in after just ten minutes in a Jacuzzi is tonic to our wretched, overworked bodies. The experts advise that if you must soak, do so for only eight to ten minutes, wear a bathing suit, and always sit on clean towels when you're lolling by the tub.

CAN SAUNAS MAKE MEN STERILE?

Studies have shown that saunas or hot tubs can temporarily lower a man's sperm production. Testicles are normally below internal body temperature, and in a hot tub their temperature is greatly increased. One study showed that a single twenty-minute session in a sauna at 80°F reduced the number of sperm cells, beginning about a week after the sauna and lasting for five weeks. Being accustomed to taking saunas doesn't appear to make a difference—the sperm count still goes down. Fortunately the sperm count eventually returns to normal if you keep those testicles away from the heat.

WHAT'S THE DIFFERENCE BETWEEN ASPIRIN, ACETAMINOPHEN, AND IBUPROFEN?

They all relieve pain, but in the end ibuprofen seems to be the hands-down winner for the most effective pain relief. Aspirin and acetaminophen have been shown in numerous studies to be about equal for relief of most types of pain (headaches are an exception—see below). But ibuprofen is at least as effective as the other two, and clearly superior to acetaminophen in the treatment of some kinds of pain.

ASPIRIN

HOW DOES IT WORK? Aspirin is a salicylate, which means it inhibits pain by inhibiting the body's production of an enzyme that allows nerves to feel pain (this is an extremely simplified explanation). Aspirin also reduces inflammation, which makes it particularly effective for treating headaches.

WHAT ARE THE SIDE EFFECTS? Aspirin can cause gastrointestinal bleeding to varying degrees, depending on how much you take. Consuming alcohol with the aspirin exacerbates the situation. Aspirin also inhibits blood clotting in some types of capillaries. Some people are simply intolerant of aspirin: They can experience hives, difficulty breathing, and other symptoms. Children should never be given aspirin without a doctor's advice, because aspirin can increase their risk of the potentially fatal Reye's syndrome. Aspirin also can increase uric acid levels, which is of special concern for people with gout or hyperuricemia. For the average individual, aspirin taken in moderate doses doesn't affect uric acid secretion. (Sometimes aspirin can be quite beneficial—see page 114.)

IBUPROFEN (MOTRIN, ADVIL, ET AL.)

HOW DOES IT WORK? It works the same way aspirin does, and fights inflammation as aspirin does. But on a milligram-to-milligram basis, ibuprofen is about 3.5 times more potent than aspirin. Ibuprofen also is better than acetaminophen at relieving pain: 100 to 200 milligrams of ibuprofen provides as much pain relief as 650 milligrams of acetaminophen, and it is clearly superior for pain associated with inflammation.

WHAT ARE THE SIDE EFFECTS? Gastrointestinal bleeding, but not as much as with aspirin. Ibuprofen inhibits blood clotting, but unlike aspirin, this effect is reversible within twenty-four hours after the ibuprofen is discontinued. Ibuprofen can sometimes be dangerous for patients with preexisting conditions of renal impairment or congestive heart failure.

ACETAMINOPHEN (TYLENOL)

HOW DOES IT WORK? Unlike aspirin and ibuprofen, which work at the site of pain, acetaminophen works through the central nervous system to inhibit the feeling of pain. It has a very weak anti-inflammatory effect, and in nonprescription doses its anti-inflammatory properties are negligible. In the relief of pain that does not involve inflammation, equal doses of acetaminophen and aspirin provide the same degree of pain relief.

WHAT ARE THE SIDE EFFECTS? Acetaminophen has far fewer side effects than either aspirin or ibuprofen. It's safe for pregnant women, nursing mothers, and children (in the correct dosages); doesn't affect blood clotting; doesn't affect uric acid; and produces less gastrointestinal irritation than ibuprofen or aspirin.

WHAT ABOUT ALEVE (NAPROXEN)?

In 1994 yet another painkiller entered the market, heralded by a $100 million advertising campaign. This remedy was Aleve—generic name, naproxen—which for ten years had been a leading prescription analgesic sold under the names Anaprox and Naprosyn. How does naproxen stack up against the other three? It is very comparable to ibuprofen but lasts longer. Instead of taking a dose every three to four hours, as you would with ibuprofen, Aleve's manufacturers claim that one dose will relieve pain for eight to twelve hours. This is a plus if you need to get a good night's sleep without waking up to take more pills, or if you have persistent pain such as menstrual cramps. For treating the average headache, however, there is no special advantage to taking naproxen, and as of this writing it costs more than aspirin, acetaminophen, or ibuprofen.

CAN A CUP OF COFFEE CURE A HEADACHE?

In many cases, yes. It's the caffeine that does it. Clinical studies on more than ten thousand people showed that both aspirin and acetaminophen provided much greater pain relief when they were combined with caffeine. In fact, the dosages of either analgesic would have to have been increased by 40 percent to match the pain-relieving power of the analgesic-caffeine combination.

These studies concentrated not only on headaches but on postpartum cramping, episiotomy pain, and pain following oral surgery. In other studies, caffeine combined with ibuprofen proved to be more than twice as effective as ibuprofen alone.

CAN AN ASPIRIN A DAY MAKE YOU LIVE LONGER?

In many ways aspirin is a miracle drug. Even the stomachache issue can be overcome if you decide to use aspirin as a preventive medicine, which many people are already doing.

Studies are underway to see if aspirin can be helpful in treating ailments such as migraine headaches, gallstones, cataracts, Alzheimer's disease, and many others. Recent studies report that aspirin lowered men's risk of colon cancer and may even delay the onset of AIDS. But the most startling and

well-documented news about aspirin concerns the prevention
and treatment of heart disease.

Aspirin has been shown to reduce the risk of repeat heart
attacks by 23 percent, and the risk is reduced another 19
percent if aspirin is combined with other "clot-busting"
drugs. Aspirin can also cut the risk of stroke in certain patients. Best of all, though, is what aspirin can do for healthy
people: In a study that tracked more than twenty-two thousand men over the age of forty, those who took an aspirin
every other day reduced their risk of heart attack by 44 percent. Because of this study, about 25 percent of healthy
middle-aged and older Americans take a small dose of aspirin
every day. One 80-milligram baby aspirin is enough to produce the risk-lowering effect. If you don't want to take baby
aspirin, you can buy Adult Low Strength Bayer, which was
created especially for this market.

What about the stomachaches? People's reaction to aspirin
varies (many don't get stomachaches from it), and gastrointestinal bleeding from aspirin varies according to dosage.
Eighty milligrams is a low dose, but if you're interested in
going on an aspirin-a-day regimen, consult with your doctor
first. Another option is buffered aspirin. This type doesn't
work well for a headache—it takes too long to get into the
bloodstream—but that's not an issue for heart-disease prevention.

How does an antiperspirant work?

Ah, the life of an antiperspirant researcher. His mission: to
discover the cause of armpit odor and create the weapons to
combat it. It is not a pleasant task, but think what it does
for humanity.

The search began with a basic question: Why do armpits
smell bad? The logical place to start looking was armpit

sweat. The pits have two kinds of sweat glands, apocrine and eccrine. The apocrine glands produce only small amounts of sweat, droplet by droplet. Eccrine glands can produce copious amounts; some people have been reported to sweat as much as three gallons in a twenty-four-hour period. To discover the origins of armpit odor, one group of stalwart researchers collected fresh apocrine sweat from unwashed armpits and proved that it was odorless (no word on how that proof was achieved). They then let the sweat sit six hours at room temperature. It developed B.O. The conclusion: The bacteria that lives in apocrine sweat causes armpit odor, whether or not the sweat stays in the pit. But it must have a warm, moist environment to grow in. (Sweat put in a refrigerator did not get smelly.)

The researchers concluded that bacteria contained in the apocrine sweat smelled bad once it had been brewing for a while in the plentiful eccrine sweat. But they wanted to know more, specifically, *which* chemical in the apocrine sweat was causing the odor. From more than one hundred chemicals gathered from men's armpits, they isolated one, hexonic acid, as the culprit. Theoretically, a substance that would inactivate this chemical would be the ultimate deodorant. But such a substance has not yet been found.

The most effective way to eliminate armpit odor, then, is to eliminate the wetness that helps the bacteria grow. What stops wetness? Aluminum compounds. No one is sure exactly why they stop it. Some theories hold that the aluminum blocks the sweat gland; or that it retards further sweat production; or that it causes the sweat gland to sprout "leaks" and secrete some of the sweat back into the body. At any rate, aluminum does not prevent the apocrine glands from producing bacteria-filled sweat. It only works on the eccrine glands.

Because Americans spend hundreds of millions of dollars on antiperspirants, manufacturers keep researchers busy assessing which antiperspirants work best. Crack teams of "sniff testers" conduct experiments that involve research subjects putting an antiperspirant on one armpit, and the product's base—cream, spray, or whatever—minus the active ingredient on the other. Cotton pads are placed in each armpit, and the subjects are encouraged to sweat. Sometimes they must sit in a hot, humid room. Sometimes they are given frustrating mental puzzles. Sometimes they are "upset" by the researchers (methods were not revealed). At the end of the sweat session, the cotton pads are weighed for wetness. The effectiveness of the ingredient is judged based on the difference in weight between the two pads. After years of such research, lotions have proven to be the most effective type of antiperspirant. Aerosol sprays are the least effective. But researchers warn that the effectiveness of any antiperspirant depends on regular—daily—use.

WHAT IS A GENERIC DRUG?

All drugs begin life as generic drugs. The name a drug is given when it is created in the laboratory is its generic name. A committee of drug experts chooses the name, and government agencies approve it. This name is not proprietary, meaning it cannot be owned by a company or individual.

However, there is a payoff for the manufacturers who fund the development of the drug. The originating company obtains a license from the FDA to sell the drug exclusively for a fixed period of time. The company may sell it by a brand name, for instance, Tylenol for acetaminophen and Valium for diazepam. This system gives the manufacturer an edge in the marketplace, allowing it to establish the product in the mind of the consumer under its brand name. When the company's exclusive rights to the drug expire, competitors can enter the market either selling the drug under their own brand names (Anacin-3, Datril, and Panadol are all brand names for acetaminophen) or selling the drug under its generic name. The competition often drives the price down. Are generic drugs manufactured at a lower standard than brand-name drugs? Some critics of the pharmaceutical industry say yes, but most experts feel there is no difference. In many cases, the generic drug and the brand-name drug are made in the same factory. However, if you're concerned about your pharmacist filling a prescription with a generic instead of a brand-name drug, ask your doctor to write "dispense as written" on the prescription.

Bon Appétit, If You Dare

* * *

WHAT IS WHITE CHOCOLATE?

As chocolate aficionados have probably surmised, white chocolate is not really chocolate at all—the government says so. In the United States, "real" chocolate must contain no fat other than cocoa butter (5 percent dairy butter is allowed to aid emulsification). The pretender, white chocolate, is made of about 30 percent vegetable fats, 30 percent milk solids, 30 percent sugar, and vanilla. The better brands include some cocoa butter, but no chocolate solids at all are to be found in white chocolate. To be fair, white chocolate has its uses. Bakers like it because it sets faster than dark chocolate yet remains soft at room temperature. It's a staple in buttercreams and cakes, and lots of people just enjoy the way it tastes.

WHAT'S AN EGG CREAM?

To New Yorkers this question may seem absurd. But the truth is that most Americans (outside of Miami and some parts of L.A.) don't have a clue what an egg cream is. They assume it's a drink. It sounds like it has an egg in it. Yuck.

What delight awaits them if they make it to the Big Apple! An egg cream is a light and frothy concoction, somewhat akin to a soda. Egg creams are usually chocolate, but vanilla egg creams can be found in some places. The egg cream was created in the 1920s in a New York soda fountain by a man whose name has been lost to history. The drink never at any time contained eggs, and there is no known explanation for its name. Two essential ingredients go into making the perfect egg cream: Fox's U-Bet Chocolate Flavored Syrup and slushy milk. Use real seltzer water from a canister; do not substitute bottled seltzer water (or, God forbid, Sprite.) Here's the recipe:

⅓ cup slushy milk
2 tablespoons Fox's U-Bet Chocolate Flavored Syrup
About 1 cup seltzer (or however much it takes to fill the glass)

To make slushy milk, put the milk in the freezer until it's half frozen. Pour the slushy milk into a chilled 12-ounce glass. Add the chocolate syrup and stir quickly. Spray the seltzer in until a foamy head reaches the top of the glass.

WHAT IS MINCEMEAT?

Mincemeat falls into the category of suspicious holiday desserts. They all hearken back to jolly olde Christmas before the age of refrigeration, when dense, dark amalgams of whatever was left on the sideboard got doused with sugar, steeped in alcohol, and served to the plastered masses. Fruitcake, steamed pudding, and mincemeat pie are a few examples.

The timeless question "Does mincemeat contain meat?" is easily answered: yes and no. American mincemeat does, English doesn't. American mincemeat typically contains raisins, citron, apples, sugar, spices, beef suet, and orange peel. *The New Larousse Gastronomique*'s recipe also calls for a half bottle of brandy and half a cup each of rum and Madeira. "Leave the mixture to steep for one month in a cool place," the *Gastronomique* instructs, "Stir every 8 days." English mincemeat is a gentler concoction, minus the meat and much lighter on the alcohol.

IS ALLSPICE MANY SPICES OR ONE?

Allspice is one spice, the dried berry of a tree called *Pimenta dioica,* which grows throughout tropical America. But it does taste like a combination of several different spices, especially cloves. Allspice is often used when just a whiff of clove is desired. It's an ingredient in fruitcakes, mincemeat pieces, and plum puddings, and is particularly popular in northern Europe.

IS RAW SUGAR BETTER FOR YOU THAN WHITE "PROCESSED" SUGAR?

Nope. There is no special type of sugar that's healthier than another, with the exception of blackstrap molasses, which is rich in iron. Honey, maple syrup, corn syrup, brown sugar, raw sugar, and table white all have about the same nutritional value. What's more, sugar from fruit isn't any better for you than white sugar. The advantage to eating an apple as opposed to a slice of German chocolate cake lies in the vitamin, mineral, and fiber content of the apple.

WHAT IS VINEGAR?

The word derives from the French *vin aigre,* which means "sour wine." Vinegars are made from a weak alcohol that can be produced from fruit, berries, melon, cereals, rice—even molasses, sugar, or honey. The most common are wine, cider, and white vinegar. Herb vinegars are made by adding herbs to any of the above vinegars.

Vinegar has been a part of the human diet since ancient times, as early as 3000 B.C. The Spartans were famous for existing largely on a vile "black broth" consisting of pork stock, vinegar, and salt. They used vinegar as we use it today—to pickle other foods and as a spice—but sometimes they used it as medicine, too: mixed with pepper and honey to treat feminine disorders, or just with pepper as a potion to revive victims of suffocation. It's easy to imagine a good dose of vinegar and pepper fumes reviving all but the dead.

Making your own herb vinegar has become fashionable recently, and it's easy to do. You should, however, follow a recipe. As a general rule, add no more than three tablespoons of fresh herb leaves per quart of vinegar. The preservative strength of vinegar has its limits, and putting in too much vegetable matter can result in botulism—not a very nice Christmas surprise.

WHAT ARE CAPERS?

They're tiny, they're intense, and they've been in your refrigerator for about two years now. . . . Do capers generate spontaneously on grocery store shelves? Are they part of some larger vegetable, or are they an itsy bitsy plant?

Capers are neither. They are the pickled, unopened flower buds of the *Capparis spinosa,* a trailing shrub that thrives in the desert. There are one hundred seventy species of capers, most of which grow in the Sahara and adjoining regions. They first made their appearance in ancient Greece, and have been spicing up dishes across the globe since at least 600 B.C.

The younger a caper is (before pickling), the tastier it will be. In parts of France, capers shrubs are set out on special sun-drenched terraces and the buds are harvested every two days, to guarantee they'll be plucked at their tenderest. Unlike wine, however, bottled capers do not improve with age. So go ahead and buy a new jar the next time you get the urge to make veal piccata.

WHAT IS SAFFRON, AND WHY IS IT SO EXPENSIVE?

Saffron is perhaps the most mysterious spice, seeming to hark back to an age of traders and exotic women in golden-colored robes. Saffron threads are the stigmas of autumn crocuses (this is not the kind of crocus that pops up in the garden at the beginning of spring), and each crocus produces only three stigmas. The stigmas must be harvested by hand; it takes more than a quarter million of them to produce one pound of saffron, which is why it is the most expensive spice in the world.

The spice has a long history and figures prominently in Mediterranean foods, especially those of Spain. It's been used at least since the tenth century B.C., when Phoenician traders introduced it to Spain and England. Saffron has always been valued as much for its color—a deep red-orange—as for its taste. Very little is needed to flavor a dish; more than a pinch and saffron can taste somewhat medicinal. Saffron is used to infuse breads, cakes, risotto, paella, and bouillabaisse with a rich gold color. The ancient Indians used it to color dessert liquor, and today saffron is used in some liqueurs as well, most notably Chartreuse.

Saffron quickly loses its flavor, so buy it in very small quantities. Purchase saffron threads (the actual stigmas) as opposed to ground saffron, which may be less pure. When you're buying, remember: the deeper the color, the better the quality.

WHAT'S THE DIFFERENCE BETWEEN SEA SALT AND REGULAR SALT?

Salt has played a huge role in history. It's been taxed, traded, even used by the Romans to pay their soldiers' salary. Wars have been won by controlling access to salt, and lack of salt has prompted the exodus of whole populations: In the fifteenth century an entire African nation had to relocate hundreds of miles to the north of Great Zimbabwe because its sources of salt had been depleted.

Salt isn't just a tasty flavor, it's essential to human life, which explains its hold over humankind. When we sweat we lose salt and must replace it either through food that has salt in it naturally (such as meat) or by adding salt to our food. Salt comes from deposits in the land or from the sea. Refined rock salt (mined from the earth) tends to be purer, that is, to have a higher percentage of sodium chloride, than sea salt, which has only about 34 percent. The remaining difference between rock and sea salt is primarily one of taste: Some cooks swear that the best grades of rock salt are more flavorful than sea salt; others say sea salt is superior. Sea salt is available in more varieties of flavor, from extremely salty tasting English sea salt to more delicate gray sea salt from Brittany, in France.

White table salt is derived only from rock salt. Some types of sea salt can be used at table, but its texture is flaky, and it dissolves very quickly. Perhaps the rarest salt comes from the salt marshes in Guérande, France, and is said to form only when an eastern wind blows. Called *fleur de sel* ("flower of salt"), it's harvested by hand using traditional wooden scoops.

WHAT IS MSG AND WHY IS IT BAD?

"My God! Vietnamese food is FANTASTIC!" If you've ever licked your chops over an Asian meal and half an hour later found yourself wandering foggily down the street with a pounding headache, you've probably encountered monosodium glutamate, or MSG.

MSG has no flavor of its own, but it enhances the flavor of other foods. It was first discovered in the Far East, and it remains a popular ingredient in the cuisine of China, Vietnam, and Japan. Most restaurants in the United States have responded to consumer's reactions against the effects of MSG by advertising NO MSG on their menus if they don't use the stuff. MSG is actually the sodium salt of glutamic acid, an amino acid found in mushrooms, seaweed, and wheat gluten.

In some (not all) people MSG causes unpleasant effects, including disorientation, headaches, and pressure behind the eyes and forehead. The red flag about MSG was first raised in the late 1960s, when Dr. Robert Ho Man Kwok traced the cause of "Chinese Restaurant Syndrome" to the overuse of MSG. The allergic reaction produced by MSG is officially called Kwok's Disease. What causes the reaction? No one is certain. But glutamic acid exists naturally in the body, with the largest concentration in nervous tissue. One theory holds that the MSG reaction is caused by a temporary excess of the acid.

In 1969 laboratory tests proved that MSG could cause brain damage in infant mice, prompting a public outcry. Baby-food manufacturers removed it from their products, and people demanded MSG-free food in restaurants. How dangerous is MSG? It's difficult to know. Our diet is made up of such a stew of additives (and those darn baby mice are so fragile) that unless you use lots of MSG on a very regular basis it would be hard to tell if it's hurting your health. To put things in perspective, salt and sugar have been proven to pose much greater health risks than MSG. And although some folks cut down on these two substances, nobody is suggesting we stop consuming them altogether.

So if you like your Chinese shrimp the old-fashioned way —with eye-popping, mouth-bursting flavor—and MSG doesn't make you feel bad, go ahead and indulge now and then. That is, if all the bad press hasn't ruined it for you.

HOW IS A FLUID PINT DIFFERENT FROM A DRY PINT?

It's a matter of volume, weight, and semantics. A dry pint is about ⅙ larger in volume than a liquid pint. The fact that the two amounts are called by the same word is unfortunate indeed, since they aren't measuring the same thing. Nevertheless, in the United States the same word may stand for a measurement in two different systems.

In the U.S., recipes measure both wet and dry ingredients by volume (that is, the space they take up, such as one cup). But measuring solid ingredients by volume instead of by weight leads to confusion when one ingredient must be substituted for another. Suppose you run out of granulated sugar and decide to substitute a little confectioner's sugar. *The Joy of Cooking* provides an example of the problem.

1 cup granulated sugar weighs about 8 ounces
1 cup confectioner's sugar weighs 4½ ounces
1 cup brown sugar weighs 6 ounces

Clearly the actual quantities of sugar vary widely. It drives cooks crazy, which is why all cooks worth their salt keep a list of equivalents and substitutions close at hand.

Recipes in most foreign countries avoid this problem by measuring solid ingredients by weight and liquid ingredients by volume, but don't look for the United States to be switching systems anytime soon. Remember metric conversion?

WHAT HAPPENED TO THE FOUR BASIC FOOD GROUPS?

Developed in the 1950s and once a bedrock of the American way of life, the four food groups today arouse suspicion. Did the meat and dairy lobbies influence the Eisenhower-era Department of Agriculture folks who first conjured up the four groups? Or is that just more *fin de siècle* paranoia? Either way, milk and dairy products now are being linked to food allergies, increased risk of ovarian cancer, and a host of other health concerns. Meat and poultry are the stars of countless news exposés that leave us mentally retching. Fruits, vegetables, and grains are undeniably healthy, unless they've been treated with some vile chemical pesticide—but that's another issue.

What do the four groups provide? It breaks down like this:

✳ MILK AND DAIRY PRODUCTS: protein, carbohydrates, fats, vitamins, and minerals. (Milk is usually fortified with vitamin D, but studies have shown that some brands are *over*fortified with it, containing more than twice the recommended amount.)

✳ MEAT, FISH, AND POULTRY: protein, vitamins, and minerals.

✳ FRUIT AND VEGETABLES: fiber, vitamins, minerals, and carbohydrates.

✳ GRAINS: complex carbohydrates, vitamins, minerals, and fiber.

There's lots of overlap, which is why vegetarians get by on only three of the four groups, and vegans get by on just two of them: fruit and vegetables, and grains. Cutting meat from your diet requires some planning, however. The protein provided by meat must be replaced by specific combinations of vegetables and grains—there's a science to it. One of the reasons meat is considered vital to most diets is because it provides necessary protein in a one-stop format.

It's an accepted medical fact that we should decrease our intake of protein and fats and increase fiber and complex carbohydrates. In essence, this means less meat and more fruits, vegetables, and grains. Because of this, the Department of Agriculture has replaced the four food groups with the "food guide pyramid":

fats,
oils,
and sweets:
use sparingly

Milk,
yogurt,
and cheese:
2-3 servings

Meat,
poultry, fish,
dry beans, eggs,
and nuts:
2-3 servings

Vegetables:
3-5 servings

Fruit:
2-4 servings

Bread, cereal, rice, and Pasta: 6-11 servings

How much is a Serving? Here's how it breaks down.

✳ BREAD, CEREAL, RICE AND PASTA: 1 slice of bread, 1 ounce cereal, ½ cup cooked cereal, rice, or pasta.

✳ VEGETABLES: 1 cup raw, leafy vegetables, ½ cup other vegetables (cooked or raw), ¾ cup vegetable juice

✳ FRUIT: 1 medium apple, banana, orange; ½ cup chopped, cooked, or canned fruit; ¾ cup fruit juice

✳ MILK, YOGURT, AND CHEESE: 1 cup milk or yogurt; 1½ ounces of natural cheese; 2 ounces process cheese

✳ MEAT, POULTRY, FISH, DRY BEANS, EGGS, AND NUTS: 2 to 3 ounces cooked lean meat, poultry, or fish; ½ cup cooked dried beans. One egg or 2 tablespoons peanut butter count as 1 ounce of meat.

Peanut butter counts as meat? Can life be that good? Yes, but bear in mind this food guide pyramid isn't measuring calories, just outlining the nutritional benefits of each group.

WHAT IS A CALORIE?

For all the time and energy we spend thinking about calories, who among us really knows what one is? A calorie is a measure of the energy food contains. In scientific terms, it is the amount of heat needed to raise one kilogram of water one degree centigrade. We require a certain amount of energy (i.e., fuel in the form of calories) to live. The amount each of us needs depends on our metabolism, the rate at which we use, or "burn," calories. If we ingest more calories than we need, our body either burns them off through increased physical activity or stores the calories as fat.

Counting calories is the most common way to gauge weight, but calories take into account only one aspect of the human biological system. Other aspects, such as the types of food we eat, vitamins and minerals, proteins, and so forth all play a part in the development of a healthy body. Because calories can be counted easily, however, they remain a handy tool for watching weight.

WHAT'S THE PURPOSE OF SNIFFING THE CORK OF THE WINE BOTTLE?

Sniffing the cork was for a long while part of the ritual performed by the sommelier who brought the bottle to the table. He would open the bottle of wine, feel the cork to see if it was dry, and then sniff it. The sommelier was nosing around for mustiness or the scent of acetic acid, which would indicate possible air seepage into the bottle, and perhaps spoiled wine. If satisfied with the cork, the sommelier would hand it to the patron or place it bottom-end up near the patron's plate. What about the patron sniffing and squeezing the cork for himself? Unless he's a very experienced connoisseur of wine, the scent on the cork won't tell him much, and he'll probably look a little ridiculous. Besides, lots of wine experts scorn the cork-sniffing routine, insisting that the cork cannot reveal anything at all about the wine inside the bottle. Sniffing corks is passé, they declare. Just go ahead and taste the wine.

WHAT IS A VINTAGE?

The word has come to mean "superior," as in, "It was a vintage year." The actual definition of *vintage:* an annual grape harvest and the wine made from those grapes. Vintage doesn't imply special quality, nor does it indicate where the grapes were harvested. Technically, all wines made exclusively from a single year's harvest are vintage wines, and all years are vintage years. Blended wines containing grapes from several different harvests are not vintage wines.

The term *vintage* began to take on meaning in terms of quality in the nineteenth century, when some wine-growing districts (the most important being Port country and Champagne) began to blend all wines except those of exceptionally good years. The good wines carried a date on their labels; the others did not. Thus, the good wines were "vintage" wines. But many wine-growing areas made no such distinctions between good and bad years: Districts such as Bordeaux, Burgundy, the Rhineland, and many others continued to put dates on their wine every year.

Where knowledge of vintages—which years were good, which bad—really comes in handy is in choosing wine produced in northern countries. Climates there can vary substantially from year to year, affecting the quality of the wine. In places such as California, Italy, and Spain, where the weather is more reliably sunny, vintages aren't as important. If you're interested in learning about good vintages, ask a wine dealer to recommend a vintage chart.

WHY DOES WINE GET BETTER WITH AGE? DO WINES EVER GET TOO OLD?

To answer the second question first: Yes, plenty of wines get too old to taste good. Modern wine-producing techniques have resulted in some wines reaching their peak at five to ten years of age, and many more may be enjoyed at two or three years. Originally, old wines were treasured because, until about a century ago, vintners didn't know how to control the tannin and alcohol levels in wine. Tannins take years to soften; thus, many wines had to sit on the shelf for decades before they were drinkable. Modern wines are forced to mature much more quickly.

Writing in *The New York Times Magazine,* Frank J. Prial put it this way: "A truly great old wine combines the subtlety of age with the freshness of youth, taking care to see that the latter does not overwhelm the former. But a lot of old wines are not truly great. They are just old. Which means they are brown in color, musty in the nose, and taste like dried leaves." Prial believes that even those wines that *can* survive thirty years in the bottle usually reach their peak at age ten.

The wine industry nourishes the old-wine mystique for obvious reasons: Old wine is costlier than young wine. In literature, films, and plays, presenting a cobwebby bottle and reverently announcing its pedigree is sure to impress the assembled group. But enjoying old wine is often a case of the emperor's new clothes: No one wants to be the bumpkin who blurts out, "What's so great about this stuff?" Besides, it would make the host feel terrible. For your own purposes, though, dust off those bottles you've been storing in the hall-closet-cum-wine cellar and drink while ye may—for tomorrow it may be mud.

What's the difference between beer and ale and lager?

All ales and lagers are types of beer. The variety in taste is a result of how the brews are fermented and the ingredients that go into them. The basic beer recipe consists of water, barley malt, hops, and yeast. To create different tastes and weights, brewers may add corn, rice, or wheat; vary the temperature at which fermentation takes place; and experiment with different types of yeast. The age of the beer also contributes to its flavor. Here's a brief rundown of the basic types of beer.

✳ ALE: Ales are made with a type of yeast that floats to the top during fermentation. They have a full flavor and are a bit higher in alcohol content than regular beer. Ales often have a slightly fruity flavor. They are not aged.

✳ LAGER: All the major American beers technically are lagers. Lagers are brewed with yeast that ferments slowly and coolly on the bottom of the vat. They are aged from one to six weeks.

✳ PORTER: A type of dark lager that is stronger both in flavor and in alcohol content than regular lager. Its strong flavor comes from toasting the malt before the lager is brewed.

✳ STOUT: An ale made with toasted malt. It is darker and stronger than regular ale.

✳ PILSENER: A pale golden beer. Light beers are Pilsener lagers that have about a third fewer calories and 20 percent less alcohol than regular lagers.

✳ BOCK: Bocks are dark German beers traditionally brewed in the spring at the beginning of beer season. They are rich and malty, brewed with roasted malts.

What's the difference between apple juice and apple cider?

There is no difference between the two, but there is a difference between sweet cider and hard cider. The juice pressed from the pulp of apples is called cider. If it's bottled and left alone, it will soon ferment and become hard—alcoholic—cider. To prevent fermentation, apple juice may be filtered or pasteurized, but unfiltered sweet apple cider also is available. Unfiltered apple juice and clear, filtered apple juice both are sweet ciders. Apple cider vinegar is made from hard cider that has been refermented and has a high acetic acid content.

WHAT IS A CAPON?

In ancient Rome, the senate hall is packed. The senators have gathered to discuss a city that is overrun, that is suffocating under an onslaught of . . . hens. They and their droppings are everywhere. Some senators fear that eventually the birds will become extinct, so unquenchable is the Roman taste for chicken. The senators act swiftly and decisively. From this day on, hens will be banned throughout all of Rome.

If such a decree were passed today, modern citizens might respond the same way the Romans did: "Hey—no one said anything about cocks." Roosters probably weren't banned because people never thought to eat them with hens around. Now gourmands turned a hungry eye to the male of the species. How to make it more plump, more succulent, more hen-like? The obvious solution was to clip its feathered manhood and see how things developed. The gelded cocks were raised indoors, usually in darkness, and were fattened on a diet of flour and milk. The result was the capon, no doubt an unhappy bird, but one that was even meatier, plumper, and more tender than the hen.

Capons are still enjoyed as luxury items. They are much larger than chickens—weighing 6 to 8 pounds to a chicken's 1.5 to 4 pounds. The flesh, much of which is white meat, is marbled and juicy. Any recipe that works for a chicken or turkey will work for a capon, but many people enjoy the bird most when it is prepared simply: roasted or baked with a bland stuffing.

WHAT MAKES FOOD KOSHER?

The laws governing kosher food and meal preparation are eye-spinningly complicated. It's not just a matter of cloven hooves, yes; shellfish, no. Every aspect of the meal has strict requirements, from the way an animal is fed to the way it is slaughtered to the dishes it is served on. The word *kosher* means "clean," or "fit to eat." Unclean, or forbidden, foods were carefully classified in the Old Testament, from which the Jewish dietary code, or *halakhah*, originates. Most of the rules involve consumption of animals. Among the forbidden are:

* Birds of prey
* Reptiles
* Any animal except those that *both* chew the cud and have cloven hooves (so no pork, horse meat, or camel)
* Any seafood that does not have fins and scales (so no shellfish, eel, shark)
* Animal blood

Eating animal meat without eating animal blood is tricky. To follow this edict, a special method of slaughtering animals was developed. The *shochet,* or religious slaughterer, must execute the animal with one slash to the throat. This makes the blood drain out faster. The meat is then soaked, rinsed, drained, and so forth to remove as much of the blood as possible. For four-legged animals, only the forequarters are considered kosher.

Another aspect of the kosher diet has to do with mixing types of food. Meat may not be eaten at the same meal as dairy products; in fact, the two cannot even be served on the same set of dishes. That is why kosher households use two separate sets and why you cannot get real milk for your coffee in a kosher deli.

During the Passover holiday, additional rules apply, dealing with not eating leavened bread. Manufacturers are eager to supply consumers with Passover-safe foods, but they've found that adhering to the unleavened guideline is not in the least bit simple. The problem: The chemical process that causes bread to rise can be triggered by a staggering array of ingredients. Not just yeast or baking powder, but a drop of moisture added to grain; corn syrup used in colas and other drinks; alcohol; vinegar; vanilla extract—all could technically result in a blip of leavening. To protect against this, food producers hire kosher certification organizations to oversee the manufacture of Passover foods.

What was the reasoning behind the kosher diet? The Passover rules can be directly traced to God's commandment in the Old Testament as the Jews were leaving Egypt. They had no time to wait for bread to rise, so He ordered them to eat only unleavened bread and to refrain from eating—or so much as touching—a leavened food during Passover week. The web of intricate restrictions that now exists results from modern rabbis' interpretations of the ancient commandment.

Explanations for the other kosher restrictions usually come down to health issues. Millennia before refrigeration, it made sense to avoid the meat of animals who themselves had "dirty" eating habits, such as scavengers, shellfish, and swine. Another theory is offered by James Trager, author of *The Food Book*. He postulates that kosher laws may have been a reflection of the age-old clash between farmers and herdsmen. The ancient Jews were herdsmen, and swine were the domestic animals of farmers. The natural antagonism between the two cultures may have led them to avoid the food of their enemy.

WHEN IS IT SAFE TO EAT SHELLFISH?

The winter months are safe; the summer months can be fatal. This is because from June to October, the algae that causes red tides can produce a toxin in clams, mussels, oysters, and other shellfish. Cooking doesn't destroy the toxins, which can cause nausea, vomiting, cramps, partial paralysis, and even death due to respiratory failure.

If the toxins can kill people, why don't they kill animals? Many fish and birds do perish from consuming the red-tide algae. But shellfish are immune to the toxins; they concentrate the poison in their bodies and can store it there for a long time. Shellfish that you buy in most restaurants or markets probably holds little risk of poisoning you, summer or winter, since potential lawsuits make purveyors of seafood very careful about the shellfish they serve. But if you're on vacation at some exotic seaside resort, and you notice the ocean has a reddish tinge, play it safe and order the salad.

WHAT IS OFFAL?

It literally means "off fall"—the parts of an animal that fall off during slaughtering. In the U.S. meat industry, the parts that used to be called offal are now referred to as "variety meats." They are: the liver, tongue, sweetbreads (pancreas and thymus), heart, kidney, brain, tripe (stomach lining from cud-chewing animals), and oxtail. In Great Britain, it's still called offal and is more likely to show up on the menu.

WHAT'S THE DIFFERENCE BETWEEN RICE AND RISOTTO?

Risotto is an Italian preparation for rice. The rice is cooked in broth and flavored with grated cheese and a variety of other ingredients such as saffron or mushrooms.

WHAT MAKES A RICE "LONG GRAIN"?

There are seven or eight thousand kinds of rice cultivated worldwide, and different categories have been devised for them. One of these is length/width ratio—rice can be short, medium, or long-grained. Long-grained rice tends to cook drier, with the kernels separated from one another. The

American palate has grown accustomed to this type of rice as opposed to shorter, "stickier" grains that many Asian people prefer.

WHAT PASTA NAMES GO WITH WHAT PASTA SHAPES?

Quick—what does fusilli look like? Who are the Italians trying to impress, anyway? Why are there so many shapes?

The Italians aren't trying to impress, they're just enraptured with pasta. Although noodles have been enjoyed around the globe for centuries, Italians are the undisputed kings of the dough. They've created an astounding variety of shapes—more than two hundred—and Italian chefs are continually coming up with new ones. The shapes are designed to complement the type of dish they are served with and to maximize the diner's enjoyment of the meal. Here is a short list of most of the types of pasta you'll find on the typical Italian menu (not including the extremely common ones like spaghetti and ravioli).

Cannelle: pipes.
Cannelloni: large pipes usually served filled.
Cappelletti: peaked hats, stuffed.
Cravatte: bow ties.
Farfalle: butterflies.
Fettuccine: ribbonlike strips.
Fusilli: squiggly or spiral strands.
Gnocchi: small dumplings or lumps of pasta.
Linguine: long, flat, narrow pasta.
Manicotti: literally, "muffs." Large tubes, usually stuffed and baked.
Orecchiette: little ears.
Orzo: rice-shaped pasta, often used in soups.
Pappardelle: broad ribbons cut in short pieces.

Penne: short tubes; the ends are cut diagonally like the nib of a pen.

Rigatoni: ridged tubes.

Rotelle: wagon wheel–shaped pasta.

Rotini: little corkscrews.

Tagliatelle: ribbon pasta made with eggs, a bit wider than fettuccine.

Tortellini: twists of stuffed egg pasta.

Tortelloni: large version of tortellini.

Vermicelli: very fine spaghetti.

Ziti: medium-length large tubes.

WHAT'S THE DIFFERENCE BETWEEN A GOURMET AND A GOURMAND?

Discretion. Pickiness. Taste. Knowledge. Put simply, a *gourmet* is a connoisseur of fine food and wine; a *gourmand* is one stop short of a glutton. Webster's kindly defines a gourmand as "one who is excessively fond of eating and drinking . . . one who is heartily interested in good food and drink." Think Henry VIII. John Belushi as Liz Taylor. Marlon Brando as . . . Marlon Brando.

And who is a gourmet? Well, anyone with the guts to declare him- or herself to be one. Most true gourmets let their admirers define them as such. In an ideal world, you would have the meal prepared by the gourmet, but you'd eat it with the gourmands, the better to stuff yourself without embarrassment.

Express Yourself

✳   ✳   ✳

WHAT DOES SEMPER FI MEAN?

The phrase is short for *semper fidelis*, Latin for "always faithful." It's the motto of the U.S. Marine Corps. Who are the Marines faithful to? Country, honor, and one another.

WHAT IS A TABULA RASA?

Sometimes confused with the **Rosetta Stone** (see page 24), a tabula rasa is precisely what that stone is *not*. It's Latin for "empty slate," and is often used when describing a situation or person without bias, whose potential is boundless. The seventeenth-century philosopher John Locke is responsible for this modern usage of the term. He put forth the idea that the human mind at birth is like a blank slate, and all human knowledge is the result of experience written on the "slate."

WHAT DOES IPSO FACTO MEAN?

Can anyone born in the last forty years read the words *ipso facto* without seeing William F. Buckley's tongue darting around his lips? It means "by self-definition" (the exact Latin is "by that very fact"). The term comes in handy when one is engaged in persuasive argument: "Anyone who denies the curative properties of Chopin is, ipso facto, tone deaf." It's different than *de facto,* which means "in fact" or actual, regardless of legal or moral considerations. Example: A *de facto* government could be one that seized power illegally but, nevertheless, is in control.

What's the difference between flora and fauna?

Flora are plants, fauna are animals. The words are singular, meaning "all the animals of a place or period of time," or "all the plants of a place or period of time." If you're discussing more than one environment or era, you'd use the plurals *faunas* or *faunae* and *floras* or *florae,* as in, "The florae and faunae in North and South America have much in common."

What does per capita mean?

It means "per person, on average." "The largest amount of land per capita of any European nation" means the total acreage divided by the total number in the population. It doesn't imply that each of those citizens actually possesses a large amount of land. Similarly, "the highest income per capita" doesn't prove anything about how the income is distributed, although it's likely that many people in the area in question would be relatively well off.

What is in vitro fertilization?

In vitro is Latin for "in glass." In the case of in vitro fertilization, the glass is a test tube. In vitro fertilization refers to a process by which an egg and a sperm are fertilized in a test tube as opposed to *in vivo*—"in the flesh."

WHAT DOES PRIMA FACIE MEAN?

This is a case of legalese snaking its way into the common vernacular, with results that can be awfully grating. It is Latin for "at first appearance," and it applies to a situation that seems obvious but may later prove to be otherwise.

WHAT'S THE DIFFERENCE BETWEEN THEORY AND THEOREM?

Theories occur in the scientific world, theorems in the realm of mathematics. A theory is a model that covers a set of occurrences in nature. To be taken seriously, a theory must be backed by numerous experiments and observations. A theorem is a mathematical deduction built upon basic assumptions.

WHAT'S A MODUS OPERANDI?

Mode of operation, or method of procedure. It doesn't necessarily imply a thought-out plan so much as a habitual way of behaving.

WHAT DOES QUID PRO QUO MEAN?

This is a term politicians love to bandy about, maybe because the Latin makes them feel authoritative. It basically means "tit for tat," but imagine for a moment a president insisting that "there will be no tit for tat between this administration and the gun lobby." In the political and business worlds the phrase implies back-scratching, trading one favor for another.

WHAT DOES E PLURIBUS UNUM MEAN?

"From many, one." This is the Latin phrase that appears on the Great Seal of the United States. The "many" were the original thirteen colonies, the "one" was the new union. Most people have noticed the phrase because the seal appears on the dollar bill. The reverse side of the seal is also on the dollar; it reads *Annuit coeptis* at the top and *Novus ordo Seclorum* at the bottom. These translate to "He [God] has favored our undertaking" and "new order of the ages," respectively.

WHAT MAKES A MEASURE DRACONIAN?

If it's harsh, brutal, or too severe for the circumstances, an act is considered draconian. The original Draco (not Dracula—although the comparison is tempting) was a lawmaker who resided in Athens in the seventh century B.C. He is credited with publishing the first written laws in Greece, and he's usually held responsible for the harshness of these laws, although in fact Draco didn't create them. He merely set down on paper the customs that Greeks had for many years lived by.

Even in ancient Greece, apparently, the printed word packed quite a wallop. Once their customs were put in writing, many Greeks were appalled at how unreasonable and punitive their system was. Even small thefts were punishable by death. If a man couldn't pay his debts and didn't own enough property to cover them, he became a debt slave. Large landowners—who, not surprisingly, were often the moneylenders—amassed huge workforces of debt slaves, while small landowners struggled to compete with them. The situation deteriorated for the nearly thirty years of Draco's reign, at which point the Greeks threw out Draco and "his" laws, canceled all debts, freed the debt slaves, and created a new, more lenient set of civil rules.

WHAT IS ANGST?

You're fourteen, and you have just realized you've bought the wrong kind of sneakers. Or you're twenty-four, and you don't know what you're doing with your life. Or you're forty-four, and you don't know what you're doing with your life. *Angst* (pronounced *ahnxt*) is psychological suffering. It's German, and it translates as "anguish." The word is sometimes prefaced by "existential," which gives it a deeper, more troubled tone. If you're suffering from existential *Angst,* you don't need the sneakers to turn you into an anguished puddle. The mere fact of existing in this meaningless world is torment enough.

WHAT IS ZEITGEIST?

The literal translation of the German is "time-spirit," which beautifully captures the essence of the term. Zeitgeist describes the cultural, intellectual, and moral atmosphere of a time and place. The Zeitgeist of America in the early 1900s included a fascination with industry and progress. At the end of the century, the Zeitgeist reflects wariness of the future and sensitivity to environmental concerns. The word is pronounced just as it looks: *zeyt-geyst.*

WHAT IS GESTALT?

Gestalt (pronounced *guh-shtahlt*) came into common usage in the 1960s when Gestalt therapy became popular. It is a German word meaning "form," but that literal translation doesn't convey the true meaning of the term. Gestalt refers to the whole of an entity, be that a person, a piece of music, or a room. Gestalt assumes that the structure or pattern of a thing is different from the sum of its parts; for example, a painting is more than the accumulation of different colors on canvas. In Gestalt therapy, the patient is treated according to his or her responses to whole experiences, rather than analyzed by interpreting specific, discrete experiences.

IS A LEITMOTIV DIFFERENT FROM A MOTIF?

A *motif* is a recurring theme in a work of art or literature. It can be a pattern in a design, a color scheme, or a dominant idea. *Leitmotiv* is a German word that translates to "leading motive." It's usually not used when discussing the visual arts. Leitmotiv refers to a recurring idea or theme, either in a literary or dramatic work or in real-life events. For instance, the leitmotiv in a play about a love triangle might be betrayal.

WHAT ARE CAHOOTS, AND WHY IS IT BAD TO BE IN THEM?

"In cahoots" is a term that originated in the Middle Ages. Germany was then rife with thieves and bandits, many of whom lived near the Black Forest in shacks called *kajuetes*. When several bandits lived together, they were *in kajuete* with one another. The phrase has survived the centuries as a way of describing two or more people who are up to no good.

WHAT MAKES SOMEONE A MAVEN?

Mavens pop up all the time on the tube. The airwaves are alive with fashion mavens, wine mavens, and of course media mavens. *Maven* is Yiddish for "expert," but keep in mind that the word is often used sarcastically: "Baseball mavens were predicting the end of the strike this week, but the mavens struck out."

WHAT'S A MITZVAH?

Driving down the street, you notice an old lady standing on a corner looking confused. Instead of leaving her in the dust, you stop, ask her where she needs to go, and drive her there. In Yiddish that's a *mitzvah*—a good deed.

WHAT'S A PRIMA DONNA?

In Italian, *prima donna* translates to "first lady," and Italians use it mostly when describing opera stars. These extremely gifted women are often treated with special care, and their temperamental behavior is tolerated because of their talent. When someone without the talent exhibits the temperament, she's called a prima donna. The term has transcended gender, and males are now routinely called prima donnas too. Is there a difference between a prima donna and a diva? Not technically: They are both leading woman singers.

WHAT IS DINING AL FRESCO?

Dining in the air, outside. In Italian, *al fresco* means "in the fresh." Ideally, that "fresh" is on the terrace of a quaint café overlooking a body of water or an old church square. All too often urban *al fresco* dining is closer to *al fumo*. Still, especially when night falls, *al fresco* has its charm.

HOW DO YOU PRONOUNCE FORTE?

You pronounce it "fort." Or "FOR-tai." Some sources claim that both are correct, while others steadfastly insist that "fort" is the only acceptable pronunciation. The "e" is a leftover from the original French spelling which, purists argue, should be silent because it has no acute accent. Thus you add the "-tai" at your own risk. The standard definition of the word is "strength, special ability." There is a forte in music, too; it is pronounced either "FOR-tai" or "FOR-tee." It means loud or loudly.

WHAT'S A LAISSEZ-FAIRE ATTITUDE?

The literal translation of this French term is "to let do." Someone with a *laissez-faire* attitude doesn't interfere with the goings-on around him or her. *Laissez-faire* has neither negative nor positive connotations; whether it's a good or bad attitude depends on the situation.

WHAT'S A RAISON D'ÊTRE?
Pronounced "*ray*-zon detr," this is a French term meaning "reason for existence." It's very widely used, approaching *modus operandi* in assimilation into the English language.

WHAT IS A BON MOT?
It's French for "good word," and it simply means a witty comment. *Bon mots* must be delivered with *savoir faire* if they are to be truly *bon*.

WHAT IS SAVOIR FAIRE?
Poise, confidence, mastery of the social graces—all of these add up to *savoir-faire*, French for "know-how."

WHAT IS NOBLESSE OBLIGE?
The wealthy have an obligation to those less fortunate than they—or so believed the French. "Nobility obligates" is the direct translation, and from this impulse have sprung countless charity events, organizations, and luncheons.

WHAT'S AN OEUVRE?
Not to be confused with *oeuf* (egg), *oeuvre* is French for a person's life work. It's most frequently used when referring to the work of an artist, composer, or writer.

WHEN IS THE FIN DE SIÈCLE?
The *fin de siècle* is fast approaching—it is French for "end of the century." Of course, throughout the century thus far *fin de siècle* referred to the end of the nineteenth century, and the world-weary decadence that imbued artistic and intellec-

tual circles at that time. *Fin de siècle* art provides countless examples of this despondent mood. Think of Toulouse-Lautrec's strident, garish cafe revelers with their sickly greenish faces, or consider Munch's *The Scream,* which was painted in 1893. Underlying the work of *fin de siècle* artists and writers was a disenchantment with contemporary urban civilization.

WHAT'S A HECTARE, AND HOW DO YOU PRONOUNCE IT?

Hectare is one of those words you see in print a lot but can't recall ever actually hearing. Its roots are French, and it is pronounced simply "*heck*-tar," emphasis on the *heck*. A hectare is a metric unit of land equal to 10,000 square meters, or 2.47 acres.

WHAT ARE FLOTSAM AND JETSAM?

"Flotsam and jetsam" is a fancy way to refer to junk, waste, or unimportant loose ends. The term refers specifically to ship's cargo that ends up in the sea. Flotsam are goods that were lost in a wreck and that float on the water. Jetsam are goods tossed overboard (jettisoned) in order to stabilize a ship. Jetsam sinks. There is a third variety of dumped cargo: lagan. Lagan is jetsam that is marked with a buoy to be picked up later.

According to maritime law, flotsam, jetsam, and lagan forever belong to their original owner, but if someone else finds the stuff, he or she can charge the owner a finder's fee. If flotsam, jetsam, or lagan washes ashore it becomes plain old "wreck," and belongs to whoever owns the shore property, unless the original owner claims it.

WHAT WAS THE ANTEBELLUM SOUTH?

Antebellum means "before the war," in this case, the Civil War. The word is usually used when referring to matters of style, either in dress or architecture. The antebellum era is considered to be from about 1820 to the beginning of the war, in 1861.

WHAT IS A QUANTUM LEAP?

The term is taken from physics, which might lead a person to assume that a quantum leap is always huge. It's not. Although there is no such thing as a quantum leap in physics, there is a quantum jump. The quantum jump occurs when an electron moves from one orbit in an atom to another. In the process, the atom either loses or takes on a photon. This change is the smallest that can occur in the energy of an atom. The point is not that the jump is large, but that it is sudden and that the electron takes on no intermediate values—it jumps quickly from one value to the other. In common usage, a quantum leap refers to a dramatic, unanticipated advance in a field, a sudden insight into a problem coming from an unforeseen direction, or an act that is an abrupt, usually radical, departure from earlier behavior.

WHY IS A PYRRHIC VICTORY BAD?

A Pyrrhic victory is one in which the heavy losses outweigh the triumph. Its namesake is Pyrrhus, king of the Greek state Epirus. Pyrrhus knew all too well the cost of martial success. In 280 B.C. he had come to the aid of Greek colonists who were defending the Gulf of Tarentum, in southern Italy, from Rome. Pyrrhus, a masterful warrior, brought with him more than twenty thousand men and twenty war elephants. In part due to the elephants, which the Romans had never before encountered, Pyrrhus won the battle. The following year he again won a huge victory, but so many of his men died that he lamented, "Another such victory and we are lost." Obviously knowing better, Pyrrhus still continued to fight the Romans successfully on behalf of Sicilian Greeks. His reward? The nervous Sicilians thought he was angling to become their ruler and forced Pyrrhus out of Italy. Within fifteen years, the Greek-controlled Italian peninsula had fallen to Rome.

WHAT IS A TENTERHOOK?

No one likes to "be on tenterhooks." Even if we don't know precisely what they are, they sound torturous. A tenter was a wooden frame used for stretching machine-woven fabric in the early days of the Industrial Revolution. Rows of hooks lined the frames; these held the edges of the fabric in place while the stretching and drying occurred. Textile makers wanted to stretch the fabric as wide as possible to get more yardage out of it. Outside the textile mills the tenters were lined up; the drying fabric sometimes straining until it split apart. "On tenterhooks" became a metaphor for feeling under great pressure or strain.

WHAT IS A SLUSH PILE, AND WHAT IS A SLUSH FUND?

In politics, the slush fund is a pool of extra money not budgeted for a specific use. Publishing houses have slush piles, towers of unsolicited manuscripts. "Slush" is a term that relates to pork. Sailing ships used to stock up on salted pork, since it could be stored without spoiling. The pork was fried or boiled, and both methods of cooking resulted in lots of extra grease, called slush, which the crew stored in vats. Evidently there was a market back then for old pork fat, because the slush was typically sold in port, and the money used to buy a few extras for the sailors.

WHERE IS NO-MAN'S-LAND?

As we all know, it can be right in your own kitchen. But in the bad old days of the Middle Ages there was an actual no-man's-land, located outside the north wall of the city of London. That is where the bodies of criminals were displayed, and since even relatively minor crimes were then punishable by death, there were plenty of bodies—hanged, beheaded, impaled—to serve as a warning for other would-be lawbreakers. Eventually a gallows was built inside the city proper. Years passed, and all around London land was settled, game preserves established, and fields cultivated except for on the former execution grounds, which were claimed by no man. No-man's-land was the term used to describe the area, and the phrase was picked up around 1900 in military parlance. It's still widely used today.

WHAT IS A PETARD?

Since you get "hoisted" with it, it must be some kind of pole, right? That would make sense if you did indeed get hoisted. But you don't. The term is "*Hoist* with his own petard," and comes from Shakespeare's *Hamlet*. At that time the word *hoist* meant blown up, exploded. A petard was a charge of gunpowder packed in metal, a sort of combination mine and grenade that tended to explode in the user's hands. The person hoist with his own petard was blown up by his own weapon, similar to someone shooting himself in the foot.

WHAT'S AGITPROP?

Agitation and propaganda, combined. The term has radical connotations, whether used as an insult or a badge of honor. Agitprop's roots are in the Russsian Revolution. The Communist Party had an official *agitatsia propaganda* unit. In the early days of the Soviet Union, agitprop was dispersed through government-sanctioned drama, music, art, and literature. In the West agitprop implies a selective use of the facts to arouse passion and support for a particular political point of view. Although the term is long associated with the left, Jesse Helms is just as likely as Jesse Jackson to engage in agitprop.

WHY IS IT BAD TO BE A PHILISTINE?

Chances are no one's called you a philistine to your face, but if you pick your teeth at the table or make loud woofing sounds at the movies, somebody nearby is probably muttering "Philistine!" under his breath.

A philistine is a loud, boorish, in-your-face individual or one who is openly derisive of culture. The original Philistines weren't any more boorish than any other Old Testament tribes, although they did produce some challenges for the Israelites, most notably Goliath and Delilah. But in the late 1600s in Germany the word evolved into a epithet. Philistine sounds like the German *Philister,* a term for "outsider." A German preacher, nervous about student rioting in his town, used the similarity in a sermon based on the biblical text "The Philistines be upon thee." Philistines became outsiders, and outsiders are *never* as refined as insiders. From there the slur expanded to the insult it is today.

WHAT IS A QUISLING?

A quisling is a wretched human being, but a wonderful word. It's the essence of onomatopoeia (when a word sounds like exactly what it is), in this case, a traitor. A wriggling, lying turncoat. A conniving, quivering, yellow-bellied . . . At any rate, the usage comes from a Norwegian politician named Vidkun Quisling, who collaborated with the Nazis against his own country. A quisling can be any traitor, but the term applies particularly to those who are part of a puppet government controlled by the enemy.

WHAT ARE THE WHOLE NINE YARDS?

"She had clowns, ponies, hats, and balloons—that kid's party went the whole nine yards." Is there some sport where nine yards is a lot of yards? If not, why is the whole nine yards used as an example of generous excess? Because the yards in question originally referred to the amount of fabric a customer purchased from a tailor to make a suit. When a tailor used the whole nine yards, it meant he hadn't been stingy with the cloth.

WHAT IS A PIG IN A POKE?

A pig in a poke is an item or an idea that seems to be one thing but might well contain something entirely different. In medieval England, small pigs were often sold at market in "pokes," which were little bags. Nothing wrong there, except that some crafty farmers took to putting a cat in the bag and trying to sucker someone into buying the "pig" without looking inside the poke. If they looked inside the poke, the farmer would warn, the pig might run away. Those skeptics who did look into the poke invariably "let the cat out of the bag."

WHO WERE THE YOUNG TURKS?

In the 1980s the media was fascinated by the Young Turks of Wall Street and the business world. The term implied raw energy and a drive to win, unhampered by fear or scruples. The original Young Turks were revolutionaries, members of Young Turkey, a political party established in Turkey in the late 1800s. They succeeded in overthrowing the old regime and establishing a constitutional government in 1908.

WHEN SOMEONE QUITS DRINKING, IS HE <u>OFF</u> THE WAGON OR <u>ON</u> IT?

It becomes clear when you understand the vehicle in question. The "wagon" in this case is the horse-drawn water wagon once used to spray city streets. A person who had vowed to give up alcohol had "climbed on the water wagon." Those who couldn't keep their vow had "fallen off the wagon." These days the colorful wagon has largely been replaced by the more arduous Twelve Steps. Either way, there's a climb involved.

WHY DO WE BITE THE BULLET TO ENDURE SOMETHING?

On nineteenth-century battlefields surgeons had to perform amputations without anesthetics. To take a soldier's mind off the pain, he was given a bullet to bite. Perhaps biting the hard metal bullet was unpleasant enough to distract the soldier, or perhaps it was just a matter of needing to bite something, anything, to keep from screaming. To bite the bullet means to tolerate something bad without complaining.

Big Science

* * *

WHAT ARE WEATHER FRONTS?

Weather is an extremely complicated area of science, a fact
perhaps reflected by the antics of television weatherfolk.
These luckless anchors must make a complex phenomenon
entertaining and at the same time appear concerned and "scientific" about it all. The science-is-fun angle on the weather
is achieved (presumably) by excited references to warm
fronts, cold fronts, high pressure, low pressure. Thick lines
studded with triangles and half-circles arc across the weather
maps as weatherpersons eagerly explain how the fronts are
moving, as if anyone really cares *why* it's going to be 101
degrees tomorrow. The real question is, How long will it last?
Weather being what it is, that question is impossible to answer accurately for more than a few days in advance (see
chaos theory, page 176).

You'll hear about fronts for many years to come, so you
might as well know what they are. A front is a boundary
between two different air masses. Since warm air rises, and
cold air sinks, a cold front occurs when a mass of cold air
pushes its way under a mass of warm air, and a warm front

occurs when a mass of warm air moves over a mass of cold air. Most storms occur along fronts, where the cold and warm air meet. The nature of the storm is determined by the temperature, winds, moisture, and air pressure in each air mass.

Air pressure (also called barometric pressure) refers to the weight of the air pushing down on the earth. Because warm air weighs less than cold, it exerts less pressure on the earth, resulting in a low-pressure area. Why does low pressure usually bring cooler weather? Because in low-pressure areas, air currents move upward, cooling as they go. The cooling air forms clouds and storms. Likewise, high pressure means hotter weather is coming. As more and more air settles downward, it compresses, gets warmer, and eventually heats up enough to evaporate the clouds.

WHAT'S THE DIFFERENCE BETWEEN A HURRICANE, A TYPHOON, A CYCLONE, AND A TORNADO?

Technically, they are all cyclones—low-pressure areas in which winds spiral inward. All low-pressure areas (even those that stretch across huge portions of a continent) are referred to by meteorologists as *cyclones* even though they may not resemble the twisters we've come to associate with the term. What we think of as cyclones are the smaller, violently intense columns that wreak havoc on land or sea. Cyclones that occur over land are called *tornadoes*. They're usually between thirty and three hundred feet in diameter, and scientists have mapped out a five-stage "life cycle" for them. First comes the dust-whirl stage (the funnel is just beginning), then the organizing stage (the funnel gets bigger), followed by the mature stage (the funnel is at its largest and most furious), then the shrinking stage (the funnel shrinks into a ropelike column), and finally the decaying stage (the funnel withers and breaks up). Most, but not all, tornadoes that occur in the western part of the Northern Hemisphere rotate counter-clockwise, and most in the Southern Hemisphere rotate clockwise.

Tropical cyclones that occur over water are called *hurricanes* if they are in the Atlantic or eastern Pacific and *typhoons* if they are in the western Pacific. These fierce storms can only develop over very warm water—the surface temperature must be at least 79°F to supply the heat transfer from water to air that fuels the startup winds of a tropical cyclone. Once the winds reach speeds of 75 miles per hour the storms are officially dubbed hurricanes or typhoons, but often winds rage much faster than that, up to 200 miles per hour. It's hard to comprehend the vast amount of energy generated by hurricanes. Consider these numbers: To spin the core of a hurricane at 200 miles per hour takes 500 *trillion* horsepower. That's the same amount of energy as exploding an atom bomb every ten seconds. Just 1 percent of the energy generated by a hurricane could fuel the entire United States for a year.

Sometimes tornadoes pass over water. These are not called hurricanes, but *waterspouts*. Baby hurricanes, many of which never reach mature hurricane proportions, are called *seedlings*. And if a hurricane or typhoon crosses over to land? It's still called a hurricane or typhoon.

WHY IS THE SKY BLUE?

Kids are the only ones who ask why the sky is blue, right? Because we adults all know that the blue sky is the result of reflected light.

What the heck does that mean?

The sun emits solar radiation, some of which is visible to the human eye. The waves that are visible are called the **vis-**

ible spectrum (see page 161). What makes colors appear different to our eyes is the length of the light waves. Red waves are the longest in the visible spectrum, blue the shortest. When solar radiation passes through the earth's atmosphere, the air, dust, and water molecules that make up the atmosphere scatter the light waves. This process is called diffusion. Blue waves, which are very short and intense, get diffused more widely than the other waves. Consequently, we see the sky as blue.

WHY ARE STORM CLOUDS DARK?

Solar radiation—sunlight—is scattered by the earth's atmosphere unless the particles that make up the atmosphere get too big. At that point, the visible light is reflected instead of scattered. Water droplets that reach this size are seen as clouds. Thin clouds appear white because they still allow some of the solar light through. The thicker the cloud, the less light passes through, and the more of it is reflected. Very heavy storm clouds look black because no light is passing through them; it is all being reflected away from the cloud.

WHAT IS OZONE? WHAT IS THE HOLE?

Ozone depletion holds a prime position in the parade of doom that is heralding the millennium. Fortunately, laws have been passed restricting the use of chemicals that deplete the ozone layer. The layer itself is a sheet of gas about the thickness of two nickels, that envelops the earth approximately fifteen miles above us. Interestingly, the same ozone that is so important in space may be dangerous at ground level.

Ozone is a form of oxygen. You've very likely smelled it—it's that pungent odor created by electrical sparks. You may have encountered it when you've been near electrical machinery or during a particularly charged electrical storm. Ozone is harmful to humans and other animals, causing irritated mucus membranes, chest pains, and coughing, enough so that the federal Occupational Safety and Health Administration (OSHA) has implemented standards for maximum allowable ozone in the air in industrial environments. Ozone is dangerous in another way, too: It can explode if high concentrations of it come into contact with a spark. Ozone does have some useful properties. Because it's a powerful bleaching agent—ozone purifies water five thousand times faster than chlorine—it can be used instead of chlorine to treat drinking water and swimming pools.

Why is the ozone layer so essential to human, animal, and plant life? Because it absorbs much of the sun's ultraviolet radiation. This radiation is harmful to plants and animals, and causes skin cancer in humans. A depleted ozone layer means much more UV radiation reaches the earth.

In recent years, we've learned how fragile the ozone layer is. It takes only small amounts of certain gases to alter large amounts of ozone. The ozone then converts to a different kind of oxygen, a kind that does *not* absorb ultraviolet rays. When people refer to the destruction of ozone, they are talking about this chemical conversion. Gases from jet aircraft destroy ozone, and so do some kinds of fertilizers. Fluorocarbons—the gases used in aerosol sprays and as refrigerants—are the biggest threat to the ozone layer, hence the new laws regulating their use.

In 1985 a group of British scientists discovered the ozone "hole" while they were studying the ozone layer in Antarctica. At that time they reported ozone levels of less than 10 percent. The ozone protecting Antarctica had just about vanished, leaving a hole in the ozone layer. The hole is as big as Antarctica itself—more than 5 million square miles. Can

scientists produce ozone in a lab, then manufacture it to replenish the ozone layer? Steven Wofsy of Harvard University
says that in order to manufacture enough ozone to fill the
Antarctic hole, it "would take three times the annual U.S.
energy output" each year. However, the earth can replenish
its own ozone; if we completely stopped emitting fluorocarbons into the atmosphere, the ozone hole would disappear in
a hundred years.

WHERE DO ASTEROIDS COME FROM?

Asteroids are small planets revolving around the sun, mostly
in the asteroid belt between Mars and Jupiter. There are
thousands of them, and more than 2,800 have been cata-
logued. For many years people believed that asteroids were
the remains of a planet that had somehow exploded. Now
scientists believe just the opposite: Asteroids are probably the
pieces of a planet that didn't quite cohere.

The exploding-planet theory has been discarded because
no one could figure out what could be strong enough to blow
up a full-sized planet against the force of its own gravity.
Equally important, the exploding-planet model conflicts with
current scientific theory. The experts now believe that planets
were formed from "planetesimals," a Muppetesque term for
small, solid celestial bodies that may have existed during our
solar system's development. Slowly, planetesimals "accreted"
into planets—that is, they glommed together and gradually
built up into a large mass. Somewhere between Mars and
Jupiter, so the theory goes, planetesimals were valiantly trying to accrete to form a planet. But at the same time, massive
Jupiter was throwing off planetesimals as *it* accreted. When
Jupiter's planetesimals bombarded the ones in the asteroid
zone, they increased the relative velocity of the latter. The
result: The asteroid-zone planetesimals were now moving too

fast to accrete. Instead of forming a planet, they smashed into one another, which is what they continue to do today.

WHAT IS THE ELECTROMAGNETIC SPECTRUM? WHAT IS THE VISIBLE SPECTRUM?

All types of radiant energy exist in the form of electromagnetic (EM) waves. The waves are electric and magnetic fields that pulse outward from the source of radiation. If you think of these as being similar to waves on a pond, you can visualize a wavelength as being the length of a wave from crest to crest. The crests and troughs of EM waves are created by the rapid growing and shrinking of the energy fields.

The electromagnetic spectrum is the whole array of electromagnetic energy. Each type of EM wave has different characteristics, and each has a different wavelength. Beginning with the longest wavelength (and lowest energy), moving up to the shortest wavelength (highest energy), the electromagnetic spectrum contains radio waves, infrared radiation, visible light, ultraviolet radiation, X rays, and gamma rays. The visible spectrum is a very small section of the electromagnetic spectrum that humans can see. It begins with red light and ends with violet. All waves in the EM spectrum travel at the same speed—the speed of light, 186,000 miles a second.

HOW DO X RAYS WORK?

X rays are part of the **electromagnetic spectrum** (*see above*). X rays can penetrate through many surfaces that light waves cannot, such as flesh and metal. For diagnostic purposes, X rays have proven invaluable since their discovery in 1895 by Wilhelm Conrad Röntgen.

X rays can't be readily focused the way light waves can, but their wavelength—and strength—can be controlled by the amount of electricity used to produce them. For X-ray images of bones, the rays are produced at a strength that will easily penetrate flesh but not bone. The ray is then beamed through the target (say, a hand), which is placed in front of a photographic plate treated with chemicals that are sensitive to the rays. Because the rays pass through flesh but not bone, "shadows" of the bones will appear on the photographic plate. These shadows contain a certain depth and detail because the X rays do penetrate bones a little bit (as opposed, for example, to the shadows cast by visible light, which cannot penetrate solid objects at all).

How do microwaves work?

Even though they've been in use for years, microwave ovens still give some people the jitters. True, you don't want to flatten your face against the oven door to watch the water boil, just as you wouldn't flatten your face against the TV or any other electric appliance, since they all emit electromagnetic fields that are under scrutiny for possible health hazards. (In the case of microwaves, it's recommended that children stand at least six feet away from the oven when it's on.) Microwaves don't "accumulate" any more than light from a lamp accumulates when you flick the lamp off.

Microwaves are electromagnetic waves that fall between radio and infrared waves on the EM spectrum. Some electromagnetic waves, such as X rays, are classified as *ionizing* waves, which means the wave can cause chemical changes in the material through which it passes. Microwaves are *nonionizing*. They do not cause a chemical reaction, but they do agitate the existing molecules in material through which they pass.

In the case of microwave ovens, this material is food. As the microwaves bombard the food, they force the molecules to bump against one another at an enormous rate, causing friction. Friction makes heat. So food exposed to microwaves generates its own heat. The reason microwaved food continues to cook itself after you turn off the oven is that it takes a while for the speeded-up molecules to slow down and stop producing heat. Microwaved food cooks from the inside out because the microwaves penetrate about ¾ to 1½ inches into the food, and the heat they generate continues to radiate inward. That's why the outer surface of the food gets hot more slowly than the inside.

Most of the warnings about microwaves have to do with burning yourself on the food: A bowl of beans that feels lukewarm on top may be steaming hot two inches down. The electrical *arcing* caused when metal objects are put in the oven isn't dangerous, it's just dramatic (the arcs may, however, pit the inside surface of the oven). Microwaves can't pass through metal, so they bounce off it, and that causes the arcs.

What is the green flash?

The beautiful and elusive green flash is an atmospheric event sometimes seen just as the sun slips behind the horizon when the last edge of the sun turns a brilliant emerald green. The flash usually lasts only an instant, but there are reports of flashes lasting as long as fourteen seconds. A few lucky witnesses have even seen bright, electric blue flashes. These are not mirages or hallucinations; there is a scientific explanation for the flash. Writing in *Sky & Telescope* magazine, Bradley Schaefer of the NASA-Goddard Space Flight Center explains the mysterious phenomenon:

As sunlight enters the atmosphere at sunset (or sunrise), refraction bends its path by about ½°. The exact amount depends on the wavelength, with a blue ray being bent more than a red one . . .

Each color forms a separate image of the sun. These closely overlapping disks appear at slightly different heights: the red at the bottom [of the sun], the orange, yellow, green, blue, and violet—in that order—each slightly higher. We generally do not see the blue or violet disks because atmospheric extinction near the horizon allows virtually no light of those colors to get through.

As the sun slips behind the horizon, the rim of red at the bottom—the first of the overlapping disks—disappears, followed by the orange and yellow disks, which are, of course, the colors we associate with the sun. Finally, only the rims of the remaining green, blue, and violet disks are left. We can't see the blue or violet ones because of the atmosphere. But if conditions are right, we can see the rim of the green disk for the second or so before it, too, drops behind the horizon.

Several factors must be exactly right for the flash to be visible to the human eye. The first is location. The sun must be setting behind a low, straight horizon in order to produce a good flash. "The separation of the Sun into colored disks happens whether it is near the horizon or not," writes Schaefer. "But when our star is lowest, the dispersion is greatest. In this case the green disk has the greatest separation from the others and forms the entire upper limb of the Sun." The horizon must be straight because "a relatively bright section of the red disk showing through a notch [between mountains] will hide the green in its glare."

The oceanside, therefore, is the best place to look for flashes. But there is another component to good flash-viewing: clean air. Smog and haze will prevent the green light from getting through. Extremely clear air, on the other hand, will occasionally allow even blue light to get through, so that the green flash is followed by a blue one. Where is the best place to catch a blue flash? "From a mountaintop looking across to a sunset behind distant mountains with a smooth profile," Schaefer advises.

Given perfect conditions, Schaefer claims that roughly one out of every four clear sunsets will flash green. But attempts to photograph the phenomenon are often doomed to failure. Even with the right equipment, exposure, and film (not to mention patience and luck), the flash never seems to translate very well onto photographic paper.

How much is 1 horsepower?

It was originally intended to be measured as the average rate at which a horse does work, but that's a little vague. One horsepower has been standardized to equal exactly 550 foot-pounds of work per second, or 746 watts of power.

Speaking of watts, they're named after James Watt, the Scottish engineer who invented an improved steam engine and also created the term *horsepower*. He needed some way to convince potential customers that his engine could far outperform the horse. By devising a system of measurement based on the power of a horse, customers could easily compare the work potential of the engine versus that of the beast.

What does the "Mach" in Mach 2 mean?

Mach numbers are a way of measuring high speeds in terms of the speed of sound. Since they measure only very high speeds, they're used only for charting the speed of aircraft. A plane traveling at the speed of sound is traveling at Mach 1; one and half times the speed of sound is Mach 1.5; twice the speed of sound is Mach 2, and so forth. The system is named after Austrian physicist (and psychologist) Ernst Mach. Mach lived from 1838 to 1916 and developed the system long before airplanes flew fast enough to need it.

WHAT'S A HEAD GASKET? HOW CAN YOU "BLOW" ONE?

Once upon a time, boys learned about automobile engines from their dads—sweating over a filthy engine block was an American male bonding ritual. Engines have gotten much more complex over the past twenty years, and fathers, according to divorce statistics, less available. And it's the rare girl who ever learned about automobile engines. Consequently, more people nowadays are vulnerable to a favorite con of car mechanics: "You've blown a head gasket. It'll be really tough to take that baby off . . . I'll have to take apart the engine." This can mean a very expensive repair bill, so it's worth knowing exactly what the head gasket is and how to tell if you've blown one.

There are many gaskets in your car's engine. A gasket is placed between two pieces of metal to create a leakproof seal wherever a liquid—fuel, oil, water—must pass. The gasket is a thin, formed sheet made of rubber, cork, paper, or soft metal. Gaskets seal parts such as the valve cover, oil filter, and cylinder head. The gasket that seals the cylinder head is called the head gasket.

The cylinder head is a large piece of metal that fits over the engine block, the biggest component in your engine. Cylinders are drilled in the engine block, and the car's pistons move up and down inside the cylinders. This makes the car move. What makes the pistons go up and down? A small explosion set off by a spark plug igniting fuel that is pumped into the cylinder. All of this takes place inside the engine block, and the cylinder head is the "lid" of the block. The head gasket fits in between the cylinder head and the engine block.

If a head gasket gets too old or is defective, the little explosions taking place inside the cylinder can blow a hole in the gasket. The results are immediate: Instead of the explosion forcing the piston up and down, it'll just shoot out the hole in the gasket. If a large hole is blown, the sound of the exploding gas will be loud, and that particular piston won't work anymore, so your car will lose power. If it's a small hole, the noise will be less intense and the power loss may be minor. (The phrase "He's really blown a gasket" evolved because blown gaskets can cause the car to sound awful.) With time the leak will get bigger, and eventually you'll lose more power and will want to get the gasket replaced. But a blown gasket generally won't result in damage to other parts of the engine, so as long as you can live with the power loss and the noise, you don't have to rush to replace the gasket.

WHY DOES ANTIFREEZE KEEP THE CAR FROM OVERHEATING?

Water is essential to a car's cooling system. No matter how cold the weather, a running engine gets hot and must be cooled by fluid circulating through its cooling system. Antifreeze was invented to lower the freezing point of water, so that a car could be parked in below-freezing weather without all the fluid in the cooling system freezing up. But modern antifreezes also raise the boiling point of water. The result: A car's engine can get much warmer without causing the fluid to boil than would be the case if water alone were in the cooling system. So why still call it antifreeze? Simply because it was developed to prevent freezing before it was improved to prevent boiling.

HOW DO BAR CODES WORK?

The bar code is a binary language consisting of bars and spaces that translates into letters, numbers, or symbols such as "$." When bar codes are scanned, the bars and blank spaces communicate the code to the computer (cash register, inventory equipment, or whatever), which translates it back into English again, conveying such things as the price or name of the item. There are four main types of bar codes, with names that smack of a John le Carré spy novel: Code 39, EAN, Interleaved 2 of 5, and Codabar. (For more about **binary systems,** see page 187.)

WHAT IS FIBERGLASS?

It's hard to imagine glass being at once strong enough to form into an automobile body and supple enough to weave into cloth. But fiberglass can do both. It is, literally, tiny strands of glass that are anywhere from .0004 inches to two-millionths of an inch in diameter. They can be from six inches to more than a mile long.

Fiberglass is made by either of two processes. The longer, thicker fibers are made by melting glass marbles, then drawing melted strands through holes in a platinum bushing. Shorter, thinner fibers are made by an air-stream or flame-blowing process that pulls bits of melted glass into tiny fibers. As the glass fibers cool, they are sprayed with a polymer that protects their surface and keeps the fibers strong.

In 1994 fiberglass manufacturer Owens-Corning announced the first new form of fiberglass in sixty years, a product called Miraflex that is soft and flexible. The company plans to use it in home insulation, where fiberglass is most commonly found. Only a few months earlier the fur had flown between the fiberglass industry and the Health and Human Services Department, which had added fiberglass to the official list of possible human carcinogens. Rats injected with glass fibers got tumors, prompting the usual standoff: Fiberglass spokesmen objected that humans don't shoot up fiberglass, while the government warned that inhaling tiny glass fibers through your nose and mouth might be dangerous. As it now stands, the EPA hasn't taken any action on fiberglass insulation.

How does electrical grounding work, and where does the three-pronged plug fit into the picture?

Elementary electronics, my dear Watson—but many of us (this writer included) view electricity with a suspicious ignorance that borders on magical thinking. If it's so important that electricity be grounded, why aren't all house sockets suitable for three-pronged, grounded plugs? How come you can use an adapter to make a two-slot socket work for a three-pronged plug? Does the adapter cancel out the grounding protection? Doesn't a three-pronged plug mean the appliance *needs* to be grounded? What is grounding, anyway?

Grounding means providing the electric current with an escape route to the ground—literally, the earth beneath us. Electricity seeks the ground, and seeks it through the easiest path, that is, through materials that are good conductors of electric current. Some things are very good conductors: water, copper, metal. Some things conduct electricity poorly: rubber and wood are two.

In a circuit that's working correctly, electricity follows a path through the wires of the circuit. When you use an appliance, you tap into that circuit and the appliance becomes part of the pathway. If something happens to break the path, for instance, if one of the wires inside an appliance comes loose, the electricity that leaks out will follow the quickest route to the ground. Let's take the example of an electric coffee pot. If the coffee pot is not grounded and a wire inside becomes disconnected, the metal pot immediately becomes electrified. If you touch it and you happen to be wearing rubber-soled shoes, your body will not be a good conductor of electricity to the ground—the rubber shoes protect you. But if you're standing barefoot in a puddle of water, you'll be an excellent path for the electricity. The instant you touch that pot, you'll get an electronic shock.

The grounding wire in a three-slot outlet provides an easy alternate path for the leaking electricity—easier than through a human body. Appliances with three-pronged plugs are grounded because that third prong is the escape route for the current. It goes directly to the grounding wire inside the outlet, and in turn that grounding wire leads back to the service panel of your building's electrical system (the metal box where the fuses or circuit breakers are). At the service panel, the grounding wire from your outlet connects to a main grounding wire, which is connected to a metal pipe buried in the earth. At the service panel, too, the current in the ground wire trips a circuit breaker or blows a fuse, cutting off the current until the problem can be fixed.

The system depends on the outlets in your home being connected to ground wires. Depending on the age of your building and the requirements of your local building codes, all of them may not be. Three-slot outlets, of course, are grounded. And many two-slot outlets are grounded as well: The grounding wire is inside the outlet and attaches to a grounding screw on the box that houses the outlet. (So why don't they just install three-slot outlets in every room? Because two-slot outlets are cheaper.) But some two-slot outlets aren't grounded, especially in older houses. These outlets are not intended for high-voltage appliances but for those that use low voltage, like lamps. The only way to tell if a two-slot outlet is grounded is to use a voltage tester.

All appliances that use a high amount of voltage are equipped with three-pronged plugs. What if you have such an appliance, but the room where you want to use it only has two-slot outlets? This is where the adapter plug comes in. Adapter plugs are those gray adapters with the green wire and metal U sticking out from the bottom . . . the metal U you've glanced at and ignored . . . the metal U that must be attached to the mounting screw of the outlet's cover plate in order to ground the appliance. If the metal U is not attached to the mounting screw, the appliance is not grounded. Or if you do attach the U to the screw but the outlet itself is not grounded, the appliance is not grounded.

An appliance that isn't grounded will still work. Everything will be fine unless a wire comes loose inside the appliance—then the situation becomes dangerous. If you're using an appliance by plugging it into an ungrounded adapter, you may be in for quite a jolt. Even when they're grounded, adapter plugs are meant for temporary use only. In Canada they're illegal.

WHAT ABOUT THOSE ELECTRIC PLUGS WITH DIFFERENT-SIZED PRONGS?

These are called *polarized* plugs. They were created as a safety feature for appliances, such as lamps, that stay plugged in all the time. Polarization has nothing to do with grounding. It allows the lamp to stop the electric current at the switch, so that no electricity flows through the lamp when it is turned off. This is important because if the lamp isn't polarized, you could get a shock from an exposed socket, or when changing a bulb, even if the lamp is turned off.

HOW DO CELLULAR PHONES WORK?

Mobile phones have been around since the 1940s, when the FCC signed off on the first public correspondence system: six radio channels broadcast from a single tower in Saint Louis. The basic idea was that mobile phones would be assigned radio frequencies that would carry the phone conversations. There were limits, however: The range of transmission from the central tower was only twenty or thirty miles, and only a few frequencies were available.

Cellular technology revolutionized the old system. Instead of broadcasting frequencies from a single radio tower, the cellular company breaks a city down into "cells"—honeycomb-shaped areas. Each cell has its own low-power transmission station. As callers drive through town, they pass from one cell to the next, and their call is automatically switched from one station to the next. Since each cell area is small, the broadcast frequencies carrying the call don't have to be very powerful—and there are many more frequencies available now. That means the same frequency can be used for several calls simultaneously as long as the calls aren't in adjacent cells. When a caller drives from cell to cell the frequency over which his call is broadcast may change, but he isn't aware of it. Meanwhile, someone across town may be making a call on the same frequency, but the power is so low that neither call will affect the other. This new technology and the greater number of frequencies have made cell phones available to everyone.

WHAT DO WATER FILTERS FILTER OUT?

A thriving bottled-water industry has evolved over the past decade, based largely on the public's opinion that tap water tastes nasty and is unhealthy, maybe even dangerous. Our water anxiety increased as news stories exposed some bottled water as bogus; standards for purification aren't as stringent as those used by municipal water districts. What is there to fear from the city water supply, and can home water filters provide a clean alternative?

There are a lot of contaminants in city water, everything from *Giardia* parasites to chemicals like arsenic and chloroform to the most common pollutant, lead. Some get in the water supply through groundwater, others are there because the water many of us drink has already been used—in some cities, used as many as five times by other people. Municipal water treatment facilities are supposed to filter out most of the harmful elements, but they don't always succeed. The different types of pollutants respond to different types of filters and purification techniques. That means municipal treatment plants must conduct a complex array of procedures to get rid of all the pollution. Like any complex system, these plants require engineers to oversee the process and fix inevitable glitches. Unfortunately, some small water utilities can't afford full-time engineers, so the quality of the water may fluctuate.

Even if the water leaves the municipal supply pure as snow, there's a chance it will be unsafe when it comes out of your faucet. That's because the most dangerous contaminant, lead, can leach into the water from underground or household pipes. Also, some cities have a hard time regulating the chlorine content in the water. (Chlorine is used to disinfect water, but it works only on certain contaminants.) Aside from tasting bad, chlorine is a suspected, but unproven, carcinogen.

Considering the fact that the quality of both city and bottled water can be dubious, home filtration systems make a lot of sense. They can filter out most of the lead (up to 99.9 percent, depending on the unit) and get rid of a number of other pollutants as well, including chlorine and parasitic cysts. The product sheets that come with the units tell which contaminants they eliminate. The National Sanitation Foundation publishes a brochure that lists maximum contaminant levels allowed by the EPA and shows you how to test your water's quality. The foundation also certifies water filters that meet its standards for eliminating lead and other elements. You can write the foundation for a free brochure: NSF International, P.O. Box 130140, Ann Arbor, MI 48113-0140.

HOW DO ANIMALS BECOME EXTINCT?

Extinction is a natural part of the evolutionary process. This fact is frequently met with hurried qualifications from environmentalists, probably because anti–"tree-huggers" tend to lump all kinds of extinction together to prove a point: Since extinction is a natural process, why bother to protect a single species? A good place to begin to understand the rhetoric is with the term *extinction*. What are the different types of extinction? Why shouldn't they all be lumped together?

Scientists recognize three types of extinction: mass extinction, background extinction, and anthropogenic extinction. Mass extinction occurs when large numbers of species die as a result of a natural catastrophe. This can happen on a relatively small scale, as when the volcanic East Indian island of Krakatoa exploded in 1883, instantly annihilating all the organisms that lived there. Or it can occur on a huge scale, such as when a large comet or asteroid collides with the earth. The dust and prolonged darkness that result from such a tremendous impact may render the planet unable to support certain types of life for a while—long enough for some species to die off. This is what many people believe happened to the dinosaurs.

Background extinction occurs when species disappear naturally from the planet. This occurs because ecosystems change even without human intervention and because some species simply phase out while others take their place. The experts have studied cases of background extinction as far back as the fossil record allows. There are between one and ten million species alive on the planet at any given time; using these numbers, and going by the fossil record, just one species a year disappears at the background rate. Knowing this helps put into context the claims that species shouldn't be protected because they'll eventually disappear anyway.

Anthropogenic extinction is extinction caused by humans. It's similar to mass extinction in that it often occurs on a continental or even global scale and has catastrophic implications for a number of species. Hunting, environmental disasters, and the devastation of habitat are common causes. It's not a recent phenomenon—according to some scientists, when humans first landed in the Americas some eleven thousand years ago, they quickly hunted to extinction fifty-six native species of large mammals, including horses, elephants, camels, a saber-toothed tiger, a lion, a giant ground sloth, and others.

WHAT IS THE DIFFERENCE BETWEEN AN ENDANGERED SPECIES AND A THREATENED ONE?

Twenty-three years ago the Endangered Species Act (ESA) was created to provide guidelines and protect species and their habitats. The ESA has two categories: threatened and endangered. A species is considered endangered if it is likely to become extinct throughout all or a large part of its range. It is listed as threatened if it's likely to become endangered in the foreseeable future. And even if a species is not on the official ESA list, it can be treated as endangered or threatened if it is similar to a listed species.

How does the ESA pick its species? Either it decides for itself that an animal is threatened, or the action is initiated by a private party. Five categories can be used to qualify a species as endangered or threatened:

1. The present or threatened destruction, modification, or curtailment of its range or habitat;
2. Overutilization for commercial, recreational, scientific, or educational purposes;
3. Disease or predation;
4. Inadequate existing regulatory mechanisms; or
5. Other natural or man-made factors affecting its continued existence.

These categories are all-encompassing, but with reason. Protecting a species is not just a matter of sending college students into the woods to count eggs, then deciding which animals should be protected on a "How-many-are-left?" basis. The labels *threatened* and *endangered* are intended to ward off catastrophe before it occurs.

WHAT IS CHAOS THEORY?

Chaos is the scientific term for the complex, unpredictable order that underlies the natural world. Chaos theory holds that systems are predictable at first, but can be thrown off course by very small events. The typical example is smoke, which may flow upward from a flame in a single plume but quickly billows and changes shape at the slightest breeze. Although the original scheme has changed, the billowing smoke does follow a pattern—an extremely complex, unpredictable pattern that is the pattern of chaos.

Chaos is not the same as randomness. Neuroscientist Walter Freeman differentiated between the two in an interview for *U.S. News & World Report*. Comparing chaos and randomness, he said, was similar to comparing "the behavior of commuters dashing through a train station at rush hour with the behavior of a large, terrified crowd." The commuters may

seem random, but there is an underlying pattern and purpose
to their movement.

Chaos theory first nudged the scientific world at the turn
of the century, when French mathematician Jules-Henri Poincaré was studying the solar system. To his shock and great
dismay, Poincaré discovered that Newtonian physics—with
its orderly laws of motion and gravity—didn't work when
more than two bodies were involved. If the universe was not
orderly, did that mean it was chaotic? Poincaré had neither
the means (computers) nor the desire to investigate his discovery. He and the other scientists of the day ignored the
findings, but the stage was set for chaos theory to emerge.

Sixty years later MIT meteorologist Edward Lorenz
opened the can of chaos again, this time during an investi-
gation of weather patterns, which are notoriously unpredictable. Using a computer, Lorenz designed a program to
simulate a simple weather system. He found that if he altered
his calculations even the tiniest bit, for instance by rounding
off a number by a small fraction, the end results would differ
drastically—way out of proportion to the fraction that was
altered. This sensitivity is at the heart of chaos theory.

Lorenz drew a conclusion that stunned the scientific community and had philosophical implications, too: It is impossible
to predict weather because an event as small as the beat of a
butterfly's wing in Brazil could cause a tornado in Kansas in as
little as two weeks. Even in extremely simple systems, only three
independent variables will render the system unpredictable.

Computers allowed researchers to dive into the mysterious
world of chaos patterns. When graphics programs were used
to help scientists visualize the chaos systems, strange and
beautiful images evolved. These images were called *fractals*,
and were explored in great depth by Benoit Mandelbrot of
Yale University. Fractals are shapes or patterns in which a

small part looks the same as the whole. They are found in every part of nature, in the branching of veins on a leaf, tributaries in a river, blood vessels in the lungs.

Chaos permeates almost every level of natural life, from the formation of clouds and coastlines to the tissues of the human body and even to the structure of DNA. The human heart itself beats not in a regular pattern but in a complex chaotic rhythm. The chaos that so disturbed Henri Poincaré appears to be nothing less than a grand biological blueprint, one that will challenge scientists for years to come.

Cyberlingo

＊　＊　＊

WHAT IS THE INFORMATION SUPERHIGHWAY?

A lot of the uproar about the Information Superhighway revolves around how much it will change our lives, and how
quickly. "What now passes for the Information Superhighway is a slogan in search of a mission," declared *Newsweek*
columnist Robert J. Samuelson in 1993. Technically, the Information Superhighway refers to the worldwide network of
fiber optic (see below) cables that have the ability to transmit
information directly into—and out of—our homes and businesses. On a conceptual level, the Highway (for the sake of
brevity) is an all-encompassing term for the interactive communications systems that are being developed for easy individual consumption.

There are two key aspects about the Highway that set it
apart from media such as books, radio, television, or film.
First, it is interactive. You are not a passive observer, but a
participant. Second, information delivered via the Highway
is instantaneous—available when the viewer wants it, not just
when the distributor wants to "screen" it.

Say you wanted to watch *The Manchurian Candidate* on

a cable station connected to the Highway. You might flip through the station's menu on your monitor, choose the movie, key in your credit card number, and wait only a few moments before the screen lit up with Laurence Harvey's anxious face. Does this mean your TV will be attached to your computer? Maybe. Or maybe both your TV and your computer will have separate means of tapping into the Highway. Eventually there will probably be PCTVs that incorporate the features of both television and computer.

The Information Superhighway will offer two basic types of fare: information and entertainment. The proponents of each type sometimes eye each other suspiciously. The information group sees the Highway primarily as an ultra-**Internet** (see below), with ever-expanding data sources, video, music, interactive graphics, even **virtual reality** (see below) programs to enhance the exchange of ideas. The entertainment faction views the Highway as a grand interactive cable channel, featuring programs, shopping, games, and anything else a consumer's heart could desire, available day and night. Either way, the consumer will be paying for the ride.

The Information Superhighway is, then, a catchall term for practically anything that will occur over fiber optic cables (and in some cases over satellite or microwave or radio). It's widely acknowledged that no one knows exactly where the Highway is headed. There are a few major destinations, though, that have people especially excited:

✳ TELECOMMUTING. Computers, videoconferencing, and instant transmission of information are already allowing people to commute to work on the Highway. As the Highway becomes more widely used, there will be fewer reasons to demand that workers all be bunched together in one location.

✳ ELECTRONIC DISTRIBUTION OF CREATIVE WORKS such as books, film, and music. Publishing companies are now wrangling with authors for electronic rights to their work so that they can convert the printed text to digital and distribute it over the Highway. But what's to prevent authors—especially those who are already popular—from simply distributing their work over the Highway by themselves and dispensing with the publishing house altogether? The same applies to musicians and film directors, and it's the music industry that is closest to realizing this transformation. Technology exists today that could enable listeners to record CDs at home directly off the Highway.

✳ EDUCATION. Interactive learning tools will offer students access to more kinds of information and more exciting ways to learn. Three-dimensional, moving video images can make complex ideas easier to understand—for instance, peeling a human body back layer by layer to demonstrate anatomy. Programs may be developed to emphasize different students' particular styles of learning. Perhaps most important, say proponents, is that education on the Highway will be fun and entertaining, and thus more effective.

✳ CUSTOMIZED INTERACTIVE TELEVISION. A key aspect of interactive TV will be that you choose what you want to watch and when you want to watch it—no more slavery to the local TV listings. What the content of all that programming will be is anybody's guess, of course, but menus will help you narrow the topics down to those you're interested in. Several software manufacturers are working the kinks out of such programs now.

✳ SHOPPING VIA COMPUTER. The interactive nature of the Highway may be a consumer's dream come true in terms of shopping for values and getting product information. You'll be able to research an item, browse through the online catalogues of dozens of suppliers, contact their reps for more details, view the item in various colors and styles, and charge it to your credit card, all via the Highway. Services, too, will be marketed over the Highway, and the ratings of consumer advocate groups will be easy to access.

✳ THE INTERNET. See below.

These are just a few of the most obvious uses of the Information Superhighway. If you're interested in learning more, ask your local bookseller for a user-friendly guide to this strange new world. *Straight Talk About the Information Superhighway*, by Reid Goldsborough, from which some of the above information was taken, is a good place to start.

What is the Internet?

The Internet is a huge international computer network made up of other computer networks. It is changing and growing every day, as new networks and users plug into it. The Internet is an important part of the **Information Superhighway** that Vice President Al Gore popularized. It connects people all over the globe; it's on twenty-four hours a day; it's uncensored.

The Net, as it's called, began in 1969 as a U.S. government experiment. The goal was to enable academic and military researchers around the country and the world to communicate with one another. Part of the motive for developing the Net had to do with Cold War fears: It was designed to keep working in the event of nuclear attack. That meant the system had to be decentralized, so that there was no Internet "headquarters" that could be bombed, thus disabling the system.

For this reason, the Internet has expanded in all directions for twenty-five years, with no one to devise rules, structure the information, or limit the possibilities. The upside is that the Net provides an extraordinarily free "town square" where people can exchange ideas. One of the downsides is that the Net can be very intimidating to newcomers. The numbers and the rate of growth are mind-boggling. In 1992 there were 727,000 Internet-registered computers; in 1994 there were 25 million.

The size of the Net shouldn't in itself be daunting—after all, the fact that there are millions of cars on the road doesn't prevent people from driving. The problem has been gaining access to the Net and, once you are on it, finding your way around. Getting on the Internet has become much easier in recent years. It used to be that in order to plug into the Net you had to be associated with a university, the government, or a large corporation that was hooked up to the system. Even if an individual had all the right hardware (PC and modem) and understood the protocols (rules and language used on the Net), he or she still had to be affiliated with one of these major institutions to get access. In the early 1990s these barriers began to crack. Now you can get on the Internet by signing on with services such as America Online, which gives you access to some, but not all, portions of the Net. You can also plug into it directly as long as your computer is equipped to do so.

What about navigating the Internet? That's become a lot easier recently, too. There are several programs available that can guide you through the waters. A current favorite, Mosaic, has been compared to the Macintosh in terms of user-friendliness. With the enormous popularity of the Net, navigation programs will no doubt keep improving.

WHAT IS CYBERSPACE?

The word *cyberspace* was invented by novelist William Gibson, who used it in his book *Neuromancer*. Published in 1984, *Neuromancer* came to be a touchstone for the new wave of young computer fanatics interested in pushing the technology to its limits. Gibson described cyberspace as "a consensual hallucination that these people have created. . . . In effect, they're creating a world. It's not really a place, it's not really space. It's notional space."

If that's not particularly clear, it's because people are often unable or unwilling to pin down cyberspace. It can be loosely defined as the community that exists between people who are connected electronically—be it by telephone, computer, or via a virtual reality system. Cyberspace doesn't have a physical location; it's in the mind. Cyberspace and **virtual reality** are sometimes used interchangeably, but cyberspace isn't only attainable through an expensive virtual reality setup. Your computer and modem will do just fine.

WHAT IS AN ONLINE SERVICE?

Online means your computer is connected—to a bulletin board service, the **Internet**, or a commercial online service such as CompuServe or America Online. Online service usually refers to one of the large commercial providers of access to the Internet. To access an online service, your computer must be equipped with a modem. It's easy to sign up for a service: All the big companies offer an array of introductory perks to entice new subscribers.

Subscribers pay a monthly fee for basic services, plus additional fees for minutes spent online. Extra options may cost more. Each service has a different fee structure, and each emphasizes different types of services. Here's a list of the basic services online companies offer:

✳ DATABASES. News, magazines, research from institutions such as the Library of Congress and the Smithsonian—the amount of data available online is astounding and far too lengthy to list here. The services' advertising brochures list all their databases.

✳ COMMUNICATION. Online services give you an online address, enabling you to get **e-mail** (see below) from other users.

✳ BULLETIN BOARD SYSTEMS (BBSs). These are online message boards that operate just like the bulletin boards hanging outside the corner grocery store (on a vast scale). Users can post messages and exchange computer files. Bulletin boards are public—you can read anyone's message. They are set up by individuals or organizations or businesses. There are thousands of bulletin boards; *Boardwatch* magazine was created to guide users through the BBS forest.

✳ GAMES. Computer games can be as addictive as chocolate cake, and they keep getting faster, more complex, more compelling all the time. All the main services offer games, but GEnie is reputed to have especially good ones.

✳ SHOPPING. Shopping online has advantages and drawbacks. The good part is that it's easy and, unlike cable TV shopping networks, you can pick and choose the items you want to see. There's lots of stuff for sale online, especially on Prodigy. The downside is that there aren't many bargains to be had, and currently there's no easy way to compare prices of similar products.

✳ ACCESS TO THE INTERNET. If the online service itself doesn't provide you with enough options, bulletin boards, and databases, you can now log on to the Internet via (at this writing) CompuServe, Prodigy, America Online, or Delphi.

WHAT'S THE DIFFERENCE BETWEEN ANALOG AND DIGITAL?

Digital technology is at the heart of the computer revolution. It's replacing analog technology, although analog still has important uses such as enhancing the quality of digitized sound and images. What is the difference between the two? You can begin to understand by looking at the roots of the two words: *digital* is taken from the Latin word *digitus*, which means "finger." Digital systems break information down into bits of discrete data that can be transmitted in a binary code. *Analog* systems represent data in a way that is physically *analogous* to the information.

An example of an analog system would be a clock with a face and hands. The hands sweep across the face of the clock in real time, measuring minutes, seconds, and hours in a continuous series of relationships—the clock's hands to the numbers on the dial. Vinyl LP records used the analog system, too: The louder the sound, the wider the wave pattern in the groove on the record. In an analog system there is always a ratio involved: The speed of the clock's hands to the passing of time, or the wide groove to the loudness of sound.

Digital information is carried differently. The book *Quarks, Critters, and Chaos* contains a simple explanation of the process:

Digital recordings . . . sample, or take bites of, the amplitude of the wave form as many as 44,000 times per second. The intensity of sound is converted into binary digits—series of ones and zeros—that can be stored on magnetic tape and computer discs as spots of high and low magnetism and on compact discs as tiny pits that are read by lasers.

It's as though the waves were sliced into tiny pieces, each of which carries a speck of sound that can be stored sepa-

rately. When all these specks are put back together, the
message is remarkably faithful to the original sound—close
to the limits of human hearing.

When you hear sound (music or the soundtrack on a multimedia disc) coming out of your computer, a sound card inside
your processor has converted the digitized information back
into analog, which produces the sound as sound waves.

WHAT IS THE BINARY SYSTEM?

Binary means "composed of two elements." Everything in
computerland is based on the binary system. This is because
computers, for all their complexity, understand only two
things: on and off. Computers assign the number 1 to electrical "switches" that are on, and the number 0 to switches
that are off.

The binary system is a way of communicating data, just
like the decimal system. But whereas the decimal system is
based on the number 10, the binary system is based on 2 or
multiples of 2 (represented by combinations of 1s and 0s).
Binary numbers are divided into standard groups called
words. Although there is no limit to the size of a word, it
must be based on 2 or multiples of 2. Most words used in
business computers consist of 8, 16, or 32 1s and 0s.

These groups of 1s and 0s don't represent just numbers,
they also represent letters and characters, images and sound.
Because binary words can be quite long, a few more terms
were created to refer to chunks of data. Since 1 and 0 can be
used for things besides numbers, they are called *bits*. A bit is
best thought of simply as one electrical switch that is either
on or off. A group of eight bits is called a *byte*. A 16-bit
word would be two bytes long, a 32-bit word would be four
bytes long. The binary system is what allows data to be trans-

mitted electronically over fiber optic cables, from CDs, and within the computer itself.

WHAT IS A PIXEL?

The visual image on a computer screen is actually a grid made up of thousands of tiny squares called pixels—short for "picture element." Each pixel is encoded with information that makes up a very small portion of the overall image.

A simple pixel, one that has only two color values (usually black and white), can be encoded by 1 bit. The more bits that are used to represent a pixel, the more depth and color the pixel, and the overall image, can have. An image that uses two colors is called a bit map, and one that uses more than two colors is called a pixel map. Not long ago, color screens were very crude: The images were choppy and jagged, the color choices limited to four. Today's color computer screens have very high resolution, which means there are a lot of pixels on the grid. An average screen is 768 lines high by 1,024 pixels wide. Most computers have at least 256 colors, and some have thousands.

The main reason color displays look so much better than they used to is that today's screen uses digital and analog technology. Pixels are stored in the computer digitally, which means that the points of light that make up the pixel can only be either on or off. A variable-graphics-array (VGA) display adapter uses an analog signal to transform the digital information into voltage levels. The voltage levels are able to vary the brightness of a pixel. With the addition of VGAs, pixels can attain enormous subtlety, so the resolution is greatly enhanced.

WHAT'S A COMPUTER CHIP?

Microchips, often simply called chips, are integrated circuits that are the basis of all computers. They're made of thin pieces of silicon that contain hundreds of thousands of electronic components which perform the on/off switching of digital technology. The very first computers, created in the 1940s, used electromechanical devices, and later vacuum tubes, to perform the on/off switching. The results were mammoth machines that weighed as much as 30 tons and had over 17,000 vacuum tubes linked by 500 miles of wiring. PCs they were not.

A breakthrough came in 1948 when the first transistors were invented. They replaced the vacuum tubes, and the miniaturization of computers began. Transistors could perform the switching function, were much smaller than tubes, used less energy, and didn't get as hot. In 1958 the first integrated circuit was developed. This early chip was made up of transistors, resistors, and capacitators (the major components of electronic circuitry) permanently connected within a single germanium wafer. Germanium was soon replaced by less-expensive silicon.

Engineers were quick to develop ways to cram more and more tiny electrical components onto the chips. At this time, more than three million components can fit on a chip less than two inches square, and industry experts predict fingernail-sized chips that will contain as many as ten million components.

WHAT IS CD-ROM?

CD-ROM stands for "compact disc read-only memory." Such a compact disc is essentially like a music CD, except that it can hold different forms of information: text, music, graphic images, moving images. Read-only memory means that the computer can only "read"—that is, display—the information on the disc; the user cannot alter it.

The beauty of the CD-ROM disc is the vast amount of data it can store. The average disc holds 650 megabytes (MB), equal to five hundred full-length novels. That's why you can buy a single CD-ROM that contains the entire works of Shakespeare, or a medical library, or a complete business resource center. **Interactive multimedia** programs would not be possible without the CD-ROM's incredible storage capacity.

How does it work? Here is a simplified explanation of a very complex process. You may recall that compact discs also are referred to as laser discs. This is because both CD stereo systems and CD-ROM computer drives use laser technology to read the information on the disc. The discs themselves are made primarily of reflective aluminum that is coated with a protective plastic layer. Into the aluminum is etched a tiny spiral track that is three miles long. The spiral track holds the information on the disc, be it music, video, or whatever.

The spiral track has two kinds of surfaces: lands and pits. Lands are flat areas, pits are bumps. These two surfaces record the 0s and 1s of the binary code that carries the information. A laser beam is directed to the disc. There the beam of light either hits a land and is refracted or hits a pit and is reflected to a light-sensing diode. The pulse of light that hits the diode generates a small electrical voltage. Thus, the result of the laser beam striking the disc is a series of pulses and no-pulses: the 1s and 0s. The spinning of the laser disc and the position of the laser beam are coordinated so that the information can be read smoothly.

How do fiber optics work?

Fiber optics use digital technology to transmit information. Sometimes that information is visual, such as a document sent by a fax machine; sometimes it's aural, such as a telephone conversation. Fiber optics can also transmit video, which uses both sound and images. Fiber optic technology is based on the **binary system** (see above): 1 and 0 are used to transmit information. In fiber optics, a pulse of light equals 1 and a lack of pulse equals 0.

Optical fibers are able to transmit pulses of light over great distances. The fibers are usually made of glass, sometimes plastic, and consist of a highly reflective core surrounded by a less reflective outside layer called *cladding*. The light enters the fiber at an angle and is reflected through the length of the core, zigzagging from the top to the bottom of the tube again and again. This principle of *total internal reflection* was discovered more than a century ago, but it wasn't until 1960 that researchers discovered a light source efficient enough to use for long-distance transmission: lasers. (Lasers—*l*ight *a*mplification by *s*timulated *e*mission of *r*adiation—are powerful, intensely concentrated beams of light that can be focused down to less than 0.001 inch in diameter. Unlike white light, which spreads as it travels, laser light travels in a narrow beam and spreads very little.) In 1970 scientists developed a glass fiber pure enough to carry the light beam without losing a lot of the light, and fiber optic technology took off. Today, lasers are used for high-speed, long-distance transmission, and LEDs (light-emitting diodes) are used for slower, shorter distances.

Two factors determine the efficiency of an optical fiber: the speed at which pulses can be dispatched and the distance the light can travel before it begins to dim (*repeaters* are used to amplify dimming light). At the beginning of the 1990s, the span between repeaters was at least 230 miles and pulse rates had reached 36 billion a second. This mind-boggling speed allows constantly changing information such as sound to be transmitted. Sound waves, whether generated by your voice on the telephone or music on a CD, are transmitted digitally via a technique called sampling (see **analog and digital**, above). The waves are sampled thousands of time per second to get an accurate "picture" of the information. The information then is translated into the binary code, which can then be fed through the fiber optic line at lightning speed. In video images, the image is broken down into **pixels** (see above), which are encoded by bits, then sent through the cable.

WHAT IS INTERACTIVE MULTIMEDIA?

Multimedia is just what it sounds like: more than one medium. Text, sound, video, and animation, in various combinations or all together, are the components that go into multimedia programs. Multimedia that is not interactive is just plain old video, a moving picture with sound that you passively observe.

Multimedia programs come on compact discs that look like audio CDs. To use one, your computer must have a CD-ROM drive. (If your computer doesn't have a built-in CD-ROM drive, you can probably buy an external drive that will work with your system.) How does the typical multimedia program work? Consider multimedia encyclopedias, the item laypeople are most familiar with. You click through menus to find the entry you want. Once you're there, you see text as you would in a regular encyclopedia. But you can also click for a still image, or a few bars of music, or a brief moving image. Usually the moving image is smaller than full-screen size or slower than thirty frames a minute. The quality of the still images vary: Sometimes they are not as clear and

vivid as those you'd find in a high-quality textbook; sometimes they're breathtaking. The sound quality is as good as
the speakers you've purchased for your system.

Some interactive CDs are nothing short of stunning in their
virtuosity and imagination. There are children's programs
that let the youngster decide how a story will unfold, and
movies for adults that do the same thing. You can take on
the part of the main character, solve a murder mystery, travel
into the future. One program lets the viewer play photogra-
pher and snap photos of pretty models as they go through a
series of poses.

Can you get really creative with any of these programs?
After all, there are only a certain number of gyrations the
model is going to go through, a certain number of plotlines
in the mystery story. The latest development in rock music,
the interactive music video, promises another level of involvement. Todd Rundgren's *No World Order*, for instance, gives
listeners the chance to completely remix his songs, play along,
delete anything. He even includes nearly 1000 sound swatches
the listener can sample and add to the music.

WHAT IS VIRTUAL REALITY?

By far the most exotic, enthralling, "sexy" offspring of the
computer revolution is virtual reality (VR). It captivates poets
and engineers alike, changes the way we imagine our future,
makes its presence felt in films, videos, music, and on the
shelves of your neighborhood toy store. Some claim that VR
is just expensive designer entertainment, while others insist
it's the next step in human evolution.

Most VR equipment consists of a head-mounted display
(HMD) and a glove fitted with sensors and actuators. HMD
contains sensors that detect the movements of the head; ear-
phones; and special wide-angle lenses that allow the wearer to

see computer-generated, three-dimensional images. The real world is entirely blocked out. By moving your head, hands, and fingers, you can experience the sensation of moving through the artificial world, picking up objects and carrying them, walking, running, or even flying through the environment.

VR could propel the entertainment industry into a Brave New World beyond Aldous Huxley's wildest dreams. If the technology gets good enough, VR could become a time-space machine limited only by the imagination of programmers, or by the user's creativity. You could play first violin in the New York Philharmonic, follow Henri Cartier-Bresson around Paris, pitch a baseball to Babe Ruth. The possibilities are limitless.

The entertainment value of virtual reality is easy to imagine, but what else will it be good for? Here are a few areas that are currently getting a lot of attention:

✳ ARCHITECTURE. Architects are already using VR to simulate building structures. Once the parameters of the design are fed into the computer, the architect or client can put on a head-mounted display and glove, step on a handlebar-steerable treadmill, and take a walk through the building.

✳ MEDICINE. VR may in the future allow doctors in different locations to work simultaneously on the same patient. Virtual reality would also be an ideal way to train surgeons without using live patients.

✳ TRAINING THE DISABLED. VR is now being used to teach handicapped children how to operate wheelchairs. The kids ride their wheelchair through all kinds of virtual environments that simulate the real world: bumps, curbs, carpet, slick marble. If they lose their balance, they'll feel like they're falling, but they won't hurt themselves. In this way the

youngsters can master the chairs in VR before trying them
for real.

✳ TELEROBOTICS. This technology was originated by NASA
for use in space, but it also can be used to maneuver in hostile
environments here on Earth: fires, toxic spills, even warfare.

✳ DATA VISUALIZATION. Virtual reality may provide scientists
with a whole new means of understanding data. By recasting
numbers as three-dimensional visual realities, they could walk
through the information, view it from endless different per-
spectives, and perhaps gain better insight on the patterns the
data holds.

WHAT'S THE DIFFERENCE BETWEEN A FAX, A MODEM, AND A FAX MODEM?

Unless you are a dedicated **Luddite** (see page 39), you know
what a fax (facsimile) machine is. You feed a sheet of paper
into a machine connected to a phone line, and the machine
translates the graphic information (the shapes of the letters
or images) into a **binary** code (see page 187) of 1s and 0s.
The binary data is sent through the phone lines to another
fax machine, which translates the data back into images and
prints them out.

Every fax machine has a modem inside it, as well as an
image scanner, a microprocessor, and a printer. The scanner
translates the image into 1s and 0s; the microprocessor compresses the data before transmission; and the modem trans-
mits it over the phone line. *Modem* means "modulator/
demodulator," and this refers to the process that takes place:
The data is modulated so that it can be carried over normal
phone lines, then demodulated so that the microprocessor can
read it and send it to the printer.

If every fax has a modem, what's a fax modem? *Fax modem* is the name given to fax machines that work through a

computer as opposed to in a stand-alone unit. With a fax modem, the modem attaches to a computer and to a phone line, enabling documents to be sent directly from the computer—no need to print out a paper copy and then feed it through a fax machine. When you receive faxes, you can either read them on screen or print them out on your computer printer. With fax modems you can't send paper documents unless you have a separate image scanner, a piece of equipment that's currently rather costly and is most often used by designers or people who deal with a lot of graphic documents.

WHAT IS THE DIFFERENCE BETWEEN A BAUD AND A BIT?

As you learned in the section about binary systems, a bit can be thought of as one electrical switch that is either on or off—1 or 0 in the binary system. Baud is a measure of transmitting data, and usually refers to the speed of a modem. It gets confusing not only because the two sound similar but because it makes sense that baud would equal bit, for example, that a modem transmitting data at 9600 bits per second would therefore be operating at 9600 baud. Such is not the case, though. *Baud* is actually a measure of how many "events," that is, signal changes, occur in one second. And in high-speed digital communications, more than one bit can be squeezed into a baud. A 9600-baud modem, then, actually operates at 2400 baud, but 4 bits are squeezed into every "event." Four times 2400 equals 9600. A simpler way to express all of this, of course, would be just to use "bits per second" (bps) and dispense with baud altogether. Lots of people agree this is the way to go, but it hasn't happened yet.

WHAT'S E-MAIL?

Electronic (e) mail is text that is carried over computer networks or via modem over telephone lines. To send e-mail you need access to the Internet, e-mail software, and an e-mail address (all of which come with commercial online services). Once you're set up, you simply write your note, punch the appropriate commands, type in the recipient's e-mail address, and click the "send" button. E-mail isn't limited to memos and short letters; lengthy documents can be sent this way as well. For many businesses, transmitting documents via e-mail is cheaper and faster than shipping or mailing them. E-mail is *asynchronous*, which means the recipient doesn't have to be around and his computer needn't be on when the mail comes in. The information is stored in a "mailbox," and the person may retrieve it whenever he or she likes.

Because e-mail is so easy and so fast, its impact on the way people communicate has taken some surprising twists and turns. Suddenly, formerly aloof individuals are more available to common folk. Whether it's the boss of your company or your favorite rock musician or Microsoft's Bill Gates himself, nearly everyone has an e-mail address. And these hard-to-reach people are more likely to answer e-mail than they are regular mail, simply because it's so easy to reply right then and there.

What about sending images or music via e-mail? Some systems are equipped to send images, but most are not. Research is under way to allow e-mail to carry audio, video, and other kinds of data, but so far this kind of service is quite limited.

WHAT IS ASCII?

ASCII stands for American Standard Code for Information Interchange. It is a code for translating English letters, characters, and Arabic numerals into binary numbers. ASCII is a universal code, which means that if you save a computer document as an ASCII file, you can give that file to someone with any type of computer program and they'll be able to translate it back into English again.

What is WYSIWYG?

What You See Is What You Get. Pronounced "wizzywig," it's a system of graphic display on the computer screen that shows documents, letters, and images exactly as they will appear on the paper. The image of the document on the screen will be the same size as the printed copy, and where you mark for a word to be italic, italic letters will actually appear on screen, instead of a code preceding the word, as in some older word processing programs. But the degree to which an image really is WYSIWYG depends upon the quality of your program, computer, and monitor. WYSIWYG is always helpful, however, in gauging things like line breaks and page breaks.

Unfathomable Miscellany

*   *   *

WHO WAS NOSTRADAMUS?

In his *Extraordinary Popular Delusions and the Madness of Crowds* (1841), Charles Mackay provides some clues to the immense popularity of the French astrologer and physician Michel de Notredame, otherwise known as Nostradamus. The sixteenth and seventeenth centuries, writes Mackay, were the golden age of astrology. It was not considered a whimsical pastime, but a serious science; even the **Black Death** (see page 27) had been officially chalked up to unfortunate planetary alignments. Amid this overheated atmosphere, in which "the devil and the stars were universally believed to meddle constantly in the affairs of men," astrologers (who often practiced alchemy as well) vied for the coins of peasant and nobleman alike. People consulted astrologers for reasons mundane and momentous. Lost a sow? Ask an astrologer when it might wander back to the pen. Planning to invade England? Ask an astrologer to chart the best date.

Astrologers and other fortune-tellers were especially popular in Germany and France. In the mid 1500s Nostradamus rose to the head of the pack after writing *Centuries*, a collection of verses "written in obscure and almost unintelligible language," according to Mackay. Nostradamus was already past fifty when *Centuries* caught the public's imagination. King Henry II of France was so overwhelmed by the verses that he appointed Nostradamus to be his personal physician. When Henry died, the astrologer retired to his native town of St. Remi, only to be recruited two years later by the new king, Charles IX.

What was so compelling about Nostradamus's prophecies? The sheer volume is impressive: more than a thousand four-line stanzas. Their brilliance lay in their obscurity, concludes Mackay. For example:

From great dangers the captive is escaped.
A little time, great fortune changed.
In the palace the people are caught.
By good augury the city is besieged.

For many years Nostradamus commanded the attention of the noblest men and women in Europe. What's more, Nostradamus's prophecies continued to excite people for centuries after his death. "He is to this day extremely popular in France and the Walloon country of Belgium, where old farmer-wives consult him with great confidence," wrote Mackay. In the 1930s people claimed Nostradamus had predicted the rise of Hitler, and as the twentieth century draws to a close, television ads still trumpet the wisdom of this sixteenth-century star-gazer.

WHAT'S THE DIFFERENCE BETWEEN ART NOUVEAU AND ART DECO?

Art nouveau came first. A young English architect-decorator, Arthur H. Mackmurdo, is considered its creator. In 1883 he published a book whose title page featured what would be recognized as the earmarks of the art nouveau style: flowing and asymmetrical, the design emanated in a wavelike pattern from one corner and spread upward across the page. Other characteristics of the art nouveau style include elongated, undulating foliage, flowers, seaweed, and so forth; whimsical and romantic depictions of humans; and a somewhat precious, extremely stylized quality.

Art nouveau marked a turning point in the evolution of design and architecture. It was the first innovative artistic movement in centuries; prior to art nouveau, designs were based on the same concepts that had been around since ancient and medieval times. Art nouveau reached its peak around 1900, although in some countries, notably France, it lingered long after that. The entrances to Paris Métro stations are some of the most famous examples of art nouveau.

Soon after art nouveau reached its height, art deco began to emerge. It was strongly influenced by art nouveau, but its goal was to meld art with science. From 1900 on, the world made great advances in technology. People were awed and inspired by industry, and the era became known as the "machine age." Art deco embraced the machine in two ways: by depicting the geometric shapes of industry, and by using mass production to create its designs.

Like art nouveau, art deco favored foliage as a motif, but rather than being depicted in flowing forms the foliage is abstract, stamped into repetitive geometric patterns. Art deco designers favored a whole new realm of motifs: icons of technology such as airplanes, automobiles, even the radio and electricity. Bridges and skyscrapers were often featured, homages to the much-admired feats of contemporary civil engineers.

The 1920s and 1930s were the heyday of art deco. (At that time, the style was known as *style moderne*. The art deco title was created in the 1960s when it became popular again.) Art deco is actually composed of three related styles. One is called *zigzag moderne*, and uses angular geometric patterns, abstract versions of plant, animal, celestial, and industrial motifs; and zigzag designs. The Chrysler Building in New York is a prime example of this style.

A second type of art deco became popular in the 1930s and is called *streamline moderne*. In architecture, it features rounded corners, portholes, horizontal bands (called speed stripes), lots of glass block, and flat roofs. The idea was that the buildings should look aerodynamic. The hotels in South Miami Beach are beautiful examples of streamline moderne, and many of them have been lovingly renovated.

The third type of art deco is called *classical moderne*, and also became popular during the thirties. It was more restrained than streamline or zigzag moderne, and featured more classical versions of the elements contained in the other two. Many classical moderne buildings had huge interior murals, often painted by artists put to work as part of Roosevelt's New Deal WPA program.

WHY IS BIG BEN CALLED BIG BEN?

First off, Big Ben is not a clock. True, Big Ben is located in the clock tower attached to London's Houses of Parliament, and the clock tower is usually called Big Ben. But Big Ben actually is the largest of the clock-tower bells. The Commissioner of Public Works who presided over the clock tower's installation in 1859 was named Sir Benjamin Hall. This tall, portly fellow was nicknamed Big Ben, and members of Parliament named the bell after him. The bell lives up to its moniker: It weighs in at 13½ tons.

HOW LONG IS A GENERATION?

Most people accept the demographer's standard definition of generation: a group of people born between specific birth-year boundaries and sharing basic, very broad cultural viewpoints. But even demographers argue about exactly when a generation begins. Baby Boomers and so-called Generation Xers are the most obvious case. Most demographers place Baby Boomers as being born between 1946 and 1964. The Xers supposedly first touched ground in 1965. But these dates are hotly contested; some demographers argue that people born after 1960 simply don't fit the boomer sociocultural profile—during the Summer of Love (1967) they were at most just seven years old.

So how long is a generation? Modern generations encompass about twenty years. Major cultural events seem to mark their boundaries. These events can be abrupt and dramatic, as when the end of World War II led to the Baby Boom. Or the events can be more complex, as when in the early 1960s Americans began having fewer children, divorcing with greater frequency, and focusing their attention inward rather than exclusively on their offspring. The children born to these folks are the Xers. In the early 1980s society's attention began to shift back toward children—"Baby on Board" signs began appearing in car windows, and fertility clinics sprang up as those Boomers who'd put off having children decided at thirty-five or forty that they did want a family after all. These societal shifts spawned what is tentatively called the Millennial Generation, who will turn twenty around the year 2000.

WHAT'S IN THE LIBRARY OF CONGRESS?

Nearly everything. The library has been called "the nation's memory," and it houses the world's largest collection of books, periodicals, maps, charts, musical compositions, photographs, engravings, and much more. Thomas Jefferson's handwritten draft of the Declaration of Independence is there, as are two copies of the Gettysburg Address in Lincoln's handwriting. Matthew Brady's Civil War photographs are housed at the Library of Congress, along with the personal papers and private libraries of many of America's most renowned men and women. The library is also home to a wealth of historical artifacts, the most poignant of which may be the contents of Abraham Lincoln's pockets on the night he was assassinated. Among them: a pair of wire-rimmed glasses repaired with a piece of string, and a packet of newspaper clippings lauding Lincoln's performance as president. In with the clippings is a five-dollar Confederate bill.

The library began in 1800 as a reference collection for members of Congress. It was stocked with 740 volumes, shipped from London in eleven trunks. By 1814 it had grown to 3,000 volumes, which the British unfortunately found very tempting—as kindling. Using the contents of the library to start the blaze, British forces burned the Capitol to the ground. The library was restocked primarily with the contents of former President Thomas Jefferson's personal library. Jefferson had planned to donate it after his death, but, being strapped for cash, he agreed to sell the 6,487 books for just under $24,000. Along with the books, the library acquired Jefferson's method of organization: Items were classified in terms of the type of mental faculty they appealed to—memory, reason, or imagination, with forty-four subcategories.

Over the years the library survived two more fires and continued to grow. It received donations of private libraries from Americans as far flung as President Woodrow Wilson and magician Harry Houdini. In the mid 1800s, it also incorporated the holdings of the Smithsonian Institution library.

Congress sporadically provided funds for the purchase of books so the library would not have to rely solely on donations or exchanges with foreign libraries.

But there is another reason the library mushroomed into the vast collection it is today. In 1846 Congress passed a copyright law which states that in order for any original work to be protected by copyright, one copy of the piece must be sent "free of postage" to the Library of Congress. The library now holds more than 90 million books and artifacts.

WHAT IS AN OX?

Would you know an ox if you saw one—if it weren't hooked up to a plow? Probably not. You'd probably think you were looking at a regular old steer, and you'd be right. An ox is neither a special breed of cattle nor a hybrid of two distinct breeds (the way mules are the offspring of a donkey and a horse). An ox is a steer, a very lucky steer.

Some bull calves in the United States are raised to breed, but most are raised to be beef. The typical bull is castrated, which makes him a steer, and is slaughtered by the time he is sixteen months old. An ox meets a different fate. He is castrated, then trained to work. Until he is four years old he is called a working steer; after four, he is officially an ox, and will spend his days in pastoral labor until he is fifteen or sixteen years old.

Although working, or "draft," animals like oxen have been largely replaced in the West by tractors and other machinery, such is not the case in much of the world. There are probably about four hundred million draft animals at work the world over, and the majority of them are oxen. Plenty of farmers prefer oxen to horses because they're calmer and brighter. In an interview with *Smithsonian* magazine, oxen expert Jochen Welsch put it this way: "You can work a horse to death, but you can't work an ox to death. It'll just stop and say to hell with you. So which is the smarter animal?"

WHAT'S THE DIFFERENCE BETWEEN CREOLE AND CAJUN?

The complex history of one of the most complex regions of America is reflected in this question. Not only cultural ancestry but race came into play as the definitions of Creole and Cajun have evolved over the last two hundred years.

Southern Louisiana is home to both Creoles and Cajuns. There are actually two groups of Creoles: white and black. The whites are descendants of early French, French Canadian, and Spanish colonists. Black Creoles are descendants of blacks who came to Louisiana either directly from Africa or from Africa via the Caribbean. The word *Creole* has its roots in Spanish: Children of Spaniards born in a colony of the New World were called *Criollas*. The French adapted the term to mean anyone who descended directly from French, Spanish, or West Indian colonists. That definition worked fairly well until the Louisiana Purchase of 1803. Both black and white Creoles identified with France; they wanted to set themselves apart from Americans who entered the region after the purchase. From that point on, to be Creole you had to be a native of Louisiana and French in culture.

What with all the emphasis on French identification, racial divisions took a backseat. Blacks with a French culture considered themselves Creole, and this didn't much bother the white Creoles. Then came the Civil War and Reconstruction. By the 1880s a fierce wave of segregationism was rolling over the South. The result: American (as opposed to French) southerners decided that since the Creoles wouldn't declare themselves black or white, they would by default be considered partly black and so classified as blacks. Under the Jim Crow laws, this had a large impact on how they'd be able to move in society. The white Creoles decided that *Creole* meant white, a notion black Creoles rejected.

While the Creoles were redefining themselves, the Cajuns had their own problems. Cajuns were descendants of Acadians (*Cajun* being a bastardization of *Acadien*), who arrived in Louisiana from Nova Scotia in the mid-1700s. Soon thereafter, the Acadians intermingled with people of Italian, Spanish, German, and Scots-Irish descent. Before the Civil War, the wealthier, more sophisticated Creoles looked down on the newcomer Acadians. To Creoles, a Cajun was a hillbilly, a slow-witted rube. Even Cajuns, once they made a few dollars and got some education, would refer to themselves as Creole. Reconstruction and racism changed all that. With the whites claiming that Creoles were racially "impure," suddenly being Cajun took on a more socially acceptable sheen. Rural whites, seeking to assert their whiteness, finally accepted the label *Cajun*, although the negative stigma attached to it would never disappear entirely.

How, then, did *Cajun* rise from its beleaguered beginnings to become a synonym for good times, great food, and wild music? In the 1960s, ethnic groups all across America embraced their roots. Louisiana Governor John MacKeithen saw the political hay that could be made from a French image—everything from tourist dollars to government moneys. The problem was, Louisiana's Frenchness had been cooked into a multiracial, multicultural jambalaya. There was no unified French consciousness to tap into. It needed to be created. This was done by a MacKeithen-inspired organization, the Council for the Development of French in Louisiana, or CODOFIL. CODOFIL put its efforts into uniting the far-flung elements of French Louisiana under the Cajun banner, no doubt because *Cajun* remained associated with *Acadian* and *white*. *Creole* was still too much of a mixed bag.

In the decades since, a well-planned campaign has been underway to Cajunize Louisiana. Festivals and businesses emphasize Acadia. The area of southern Louisiana was officially named Acadiana. But the most effective force of change has been the career of flamboyant Governor Edwin Edwards, who ran for office as a Cajun in the early 1970s and held his post until the mid-1990s. In the intervening years, Cajun has come to include everyone who resides in Louisiana and claims a French heritage or culture. To the rest of America, Louisiana is now Cajun Country.

The Creoles and Cajuns themselves still feel culturally distinct from each other, but not to the same degree they once did. The public relations campaign of CODOFIL seems to be working in terms of pulling more whites into the Cajun circle. Blacks, however, continue to identify themselves as Creole and to consider Cajuns to be exclusively white.

WHAT MAKES A VIRGIN VESTAL?

The term *vestal virgin* conjures up images of the ultimate virgin, one who is even more virginal than a regular virgin. It seems likely that she'd perform her secret purifying rites during Vespers, which means vestal virgins are probably Catholic.

Not exactly. In fact, vestal virgins were around before Christ was born. Vesta, the Roman goddess the virgins honored, was the oldest daughter of Saturn. She never married, but dedicated herself to hearth and home. Vesta evolved into quite the matriarch, commanding a circular temple that stood in the center of Rome. Every Roman house had a shrine to Vesta, and every meal began and ended with an offering to Vesta.

The virgins were actually priestesses who kept watch over a sacred fire that burned in Vesta's temple. The custom began in primitive times, when fires were difficult to make. People would obtain fire from the local chief, whose daughters kept a flame burning at all times. Eventually fire making became routine, but the vestal virgins must have appealed to the Romans, who kept six virgins posted in Vesta's temple round the clock, keeping the city's home fire aglow.

WHAT IS THE FORMULA IN A FORMULA RACE CAR?

There are several formulas, but the most glamorous is the Formula One race car. Formula Two and Formula Three cars do exist, but you won't find slinky European model-actresses hanging around the drivers of those. Formula Two and Three cars are used to train future Formula One drivers.

The formula itself is a set of technical specifications to which the car must adhere. Each Formula One car is individually designed and manufactured. The design has a lot in common with airplane design: Like the fuselage of an airplane, the Formula One car is basically a single tube that supports the engine and suspension system. The car even has front and rear wings. When the car is moving, the flow of air past these wings produces a downforce that pushes the car to the road, enabling it to go around curves faster.

Grand Prix cars and Formula One cars are the same thing. Formula One cars compete in the Grand Prix, a series of about fifteen races held around the world. The cars reach speeds of more than 200 miles per hour, tearing over the roads of Europe and Latin America. The United States isn't as keen on hosting these events—the road races are too often a formula for accidents and lawsuits.

WHAT'S THE DIFFERENCE BETWEEN A DWARF AND A MIDGET?

There's something that feels politically incorrect about this question, which is why it's included in this book; you probably won't have the opportunity or nerve to ask a little person in person. *Little person* is the socially acceptable term for dwarf. *Dwarf* is the medical term, and *midget* is simply not used—it's considered very offensive. Nevertheless, there are certain commonly recognized physical differences between dwarfs and "midgets."

There are more than one hundred types of dwarfism. Clinically, a dwarf is someone who is four feet ten inches or shorter. No one knows exactly how many dwarfs reside in the United States; estimates range from twenty thousand to one hundred thousand. Most dwarfs have a condition called *chondrodystrophy*, which results in the body growing disproportionately: It is shorter than average, and the limbs are small in proportion to the torso and head.

Some people become dwarfs when a malfunction of the pituitary gland prevents their bodies from producing enough growth hormone. These dwarfs are short, but their bodies are correctly proportioned; they look like very small men and women. These are the people who in the past have been called midgets. In medical parlance, they are *hypopituitary* dwarfs. Nowadays this condition can be treated with growth hormones.

Little people are understandably weary of the mystical haze through which they've been viewed for centuries. Magical miniature creatures—be they called leprechauns, fairies, elves, or whatever—appear in tales from ancient Egypt, Greece, Rome, even Mayan and other South American cultures. And of course, they are frequent players in European folklore. Before the genetic components of dwarfism were understood, dwarfs were generally believed to possess supernatural powers or be symbols of Mother Nature's playfulness. Accordingly, dwarfs existed in different cultures as deities, jesters, acrobats, and so forth. In the Middle Ages they were employed as jewel keep-

ers; it would be impossible for them to abscond with the
jewels because they could never blend into a crowd. But always, dwarfs were kept somewhat outside the mainstream of
society.

A particularly demeaning role for dwarfs has been a relatively modern one: carnival sideshow attraction. First exhib-
ited in traveling fairs in nineteenth-century England and
America, dwarfs were billed as freaks of nature and held in
cages. The dwarf later "graduated" to being a comic per-
former in the circus. Circuses traditionally called little people
midgets, which is why the word is now considered a slur.

WHAT ARE THE MASONS?

There are about 5.5 million Masons worldwide, of which 4.5
million reside in the United States. In a 1993 Mason publication, R. Stephen Doan offered a fascinating history of the
mysterious fraternal brotherhood.

The Masons began as a group of stonemasons who organized in the Middle Ages to teach the architectural secrets of
building Gothic cathedrals. Gothic architecture was a drastically innovative style of design. Its origins are uncertain, but it
may have been borrowed from Arab architecture and brought
to Europe by Crusaders returning from the Holy Land. Up until the Gothic era, buildings were constructed with thick walls
and columns to support the weight of a roof or upper stories.
Gothic architecture relied instead on counterbalanced forces.
The pointed Gothic arches direct weight diagonally away
from the arch. When two arches are placed next to each
other, the downward pressure from one supports the downward pressure from the other. The result: Walls could be thinner and could soar to the heavens—sometimes as high as
forty stories. The world had never seen structures this tall
and wouldn't see them again for many centuries.

Who held the secrets to creating these glorious cathedrals? The stonemasons who built them. These stonemasons had a monopoly on the technique and wanted to keep it that way. The cathedral business was booming by the late 1200s, and many new stonemasons were needed to fill the demand. The best way for the master stonemasons to control the trade was to form a brotherhood and regulate who got to apprentice and eventually become a practitioner of the craft.

"The craftsmen of these early days left no plans or drawings," writes Doan. ". . . The secrets of their art were transmitted orally, learned by example, and closely guarded. . . . Because of the possibility of accident and therefore death or disability of members of the craft, the ancient brothers provided for relief or charity for those distressed members of their order." Here are the seeds of the philosophy that guide modern-day Masons: brotherly love, relief or charity, truth, temperance, fortitude, prudence, and justice. But how did the organization grow from a group of secretive stonemasons to a group of secretive guys in funny hats?

Eventually the cathedral-building boom went bust. All the towns that could afford to construct and maintain a cathedral had one. Meanwhile, ordinary citizens had become intrigued by the Masons' philosophy. Around 1600, the Masons began to accept members who were not actual stonemasons. The term "free and accepted Masons" was used when referring to these members, and it is still used today, usually shortened to "freemason."

The Masons fervently nourished secrecy and ritual. Secret oaths have always existed, and the secret greeting (the Masonic "word") is first documented in Scotland around 1550. At the close of the twentieth century, there are more than one thousand Masonic degrees that members can obtain, accompanied by some one hundred rites. Most members complete only the first three degrees: Entered Apprentice, Fellowcraft, and Master Mason. For those who wish to go onward and upward in the hierarchy, titles include Sublime Master Elected, Prince of Libanus, and Knight of the Brazen Serpent, to name only a few.

What about those hats? The hats aren't worn by all Masons, only by Shriners. The Shriners are an auxiliary order of Masons. There are at least fifty such auxiliaries, some for women. The Shriners' full name, by the way, is Ancient Arabic Order of the Nobles of the Mystic Shrine. You must be a 32nd-degree Mason to be accepted as a Shriner. The group has always emphasized colorful regalia and mass ceremonials (hence their frequent appearance in parades), but more notable is their support of nearly two dozen hospitals for crippled children. A child need only be recommended by a Mason to receive free treatment at one of the hospitals.

WHY ARE MOST PEOPLE RIGHT-HANDED?

No creature besides man exhibits a preference for one hand (or paw or claw) across the entire species. Individual animals may prefer one paw to another, but they are easily swayed by variables such as the placement of an object they're reaching for. Human beings, however, are dextral (right-handed) all over the world, in all races and cultures. Scientists have long tried to discover why.

Most researchers now believe that it has something to do with the development of fine motor skills in human beings, and the way the brain controls those skills. Originally, it was thought that because the left side of the brain controlled speech, it controlled all the higher functions, including skills like writing. Scientists then discovered that the right side plays an important role in higher functions, too, especially those involving spatial perception, reasoning, and memory.

The two sides of the brain complement each other; neither is in sole command of "superior" functions. But there is a striking difference between the two hemispheres that may account for right-handedness: Research suggests that in right-handers, the left side of the brain has sensory and motor connections to both sides of the body; the right side of the brain does not. In terms of sensory and motor connections, the right side of the brain is plugged in only to the left side of the body.

What this means is that the left side of the brain probably has the job of *integrating* activity on both sides of the body, so that we can smoothly perform various actions. If this is true, it makes sense that it is easier for most people to use the right hand, because it is controlled by the side of the brain that integrates all the activities needed for fine motor skills.

There also is a link between speech and right-handedness. The neural motor systems of speech and of the right hand are adjacent. The right hand is the one most people use for gesturing as they are talking; that is, it is used for communication as well as for fine motor skills. We gesticulate when we talk, but not when we do other activities such as listening to music or riding a stationary bike. As further evidence of the connection, researchers have found that talking disturbs a person's ability to coordinate movements with the right hand. Studies show that it is far more difficult to balance a rod on one finger of the right hand while talking than it is to balance a rod on a finger of the left hand.

But what about left-handers? There is still much uncertainty about why they develop that way. Some of them have speech centers on the right side of the brain, but many do not. Left-handers are as adept at using their chosen hand as right-handers are. There is a lot of disagreement about how many lefties are out there: Estimates range from 4 to 36 percent of the human race. They've been in the minority since the dawn of recorded history, and like all minorities, they've suffered for it. Left-handers are called "sinistrals" (from the Latin *sinistr*, meaning "left, on the left side, unfavorable"), and the left has long been associated with evil, witchcraft, impurity, and uncleanliness. As recently as a few decades ago, left-handed children were forced to write with their right hand. Although left-handedness is still little understood, at least society seems to have outgrown its prejudices about the phenomenon.

ARE SPONGES PLANTS OR ANIMALS?

Okay, so it's not a pressing question, but still it's a colorful tidbit of information. Sponges are animals. The sponges we use are actually the skeletons of sponges. The animals are pulled from the sea, hung to dry, and then washed and treated until they're ready for market. If it sounds a little gruesome, bear in mind that sponges don't resemble what we usually think of as animals: They have neither head nor mouth nor internal organs. The entire sponge consists of a series of water canals that bring in food and oxygen and carry away waste.

Most store-bought sponges aren't real sponges at all, but synthetic material designed to look like the real thing. Natural sea sponges are gradually becoming luxury items because they must be harvested by hand. Harvesting sponges goes back thousands of years and is not without its dangers. Sickness, disability, and the bends plague the sponge fishermen, some of whom dive to depths of two hundred feet in search of their prey. Although modern scuba equipment has made the work somewhat easier, it's a dying art in many parts of the world.

WHAT IS POSTMODERNISM?

The term is used most often in architecture, but its influence in contemporary thought reaches far beyond that realm. From an architectural perspective, postmodernism is a reaction to modernism, the branch of building design begun in post–World War I Germany as the Bauhaus movement. It featured flat angles, no ornamentation, plate glass, concrete, and heavy use of functional, "working-class" materials. Gaze at any urban skyline and you'll see plenty of examples of the modern style (buildings that predate the modern era, such as the Empire State Building or the Chrysler Building, offer a welcome contrast). Modern structures were conceived in part as a reaction to the hated middle class—the bourgeoisie—of the European nations from which the modern architects sprang. Bourgeois sensibilities were petty and frivolous, just like the cornices, gargoyles, fluted columns, and other superfluous decorations on their buildings. Modernism was pure, clean, oriented toward the worker, not the worker's wasteful middle-class boss.

Although a glance at new high-rise construction going on in your burg will confirm that modernism is still alive and kicking, it "officially" was killed off at 3:32 P.M. on July 15, 1972. At that hour the Pruitt-Igoe housing development in Saint Louis was dynamited to the ground, on charges that it was uninhabitable. The "machine for living" as developed by Le Corbusier and other "high modernists" had finally fallen from grace. But what was to replace it?

The answer is postmodernism, but postmodernism does not signify a specific school of design. The term was created in the mid-1970s by Charles Jencks. "The term Post-Modernism caught on as the name for all developments since the general exhaustion of modernism itself," writes Tom Wolfe in *From Bauhaus to Our House*. "The new term tended to create the impression that modernism was over because it had been superseded by something new. . . . In fact, the Post-Modernists had never emerged from the spare little box fashioned in the 1920s." This is still basically true today. No new, unified school of design has developed, although contemporary architects do tend to embellish the outside of their buildings more than the modernists did, often using playful, nonfunctional versions of classical elements. The classical elements aren't necessary for a building to be considered postmodern, though: Postmodernism is anything that isn't strictly modern. There are no parameters.

In the area of social science, postmodernism describes the falling-apart-at-the-seams feeling hanging over the last quarter of the twentieth century. To get a sense of the weight and meaning of this theory, you need to understand what came before it.

Postmodernism is a way of viewing social structures. Before postmodernism there was modernism; before modernism there was religion. In religious society, the word of God created the structure by which humans lived. Although powerful people interpreted God's word in ways that best suited their own ends, human existence nevertheless revolved around belief in a "received order." Christian (or Jewish or Muslim) law circumscribed every inch of a person's inner and outer life. A higher order had developed this law; it was beyond human hands. The great thinkers of the modern era, which began roughly around the mid 1800s, broke with this world view. In the periodical *boundary 2*, Norbert Lechner explains that

[modernity is a] slow transition from a *received order* to a *produced order*. The emphasis is double. On one side, the social *production* of order: The world ceases to be a predetermined system that we must submit to and becomes the object of human will. . . . On the other side, *order* itself: There is no longer an absolute law nor a sacred tradition that prosecutes human will, and it is humankind that has to limit itself.

Humans responded to this terrifying but exhilarating challenge by trying to create social systems that would be as all-encompassing as God's word had been. They were used to a total system that provided a reference point for everything: values, loyalties, behavior, priorities, family, war. Some of the modern systems that evolved to meet this need were democracy, communism, and nationalism. (Democracy and nationalism had existed earlier, but they were not expected to cover as much ground—when one fought for "God and country," God came first. In contrast, in this century U.S. citizens have been urged to fight for democracy and the "American way of life.")

The modern systems attempted to force all aspects of human possibility into a single unified theory, but human nature is too complex for that. Enter postmodernism, which, says Lechner, is "the loss of faith in the possibility of a theory that possesses the key to understanding social process in its entirety." If it's daunting to think we must create a social system to replace God's law, it's deeply disturbing to realize that such a system is probably not possible. The resurgence of fundamentalist religions could be viewed as a reaction to the postmodern dilemma—an attempt to squeeze the contemporary world into a system that can provide all the answers.

For those who accept the postmodern view, Lechner offers an intriguing glimmer of light: Has the search for a unified system been abandoned "because it is not possible or because it is no longer necessary"? Perhaps out of the diversity and chaos of the postmodern era a new, more flexible social system will blossom. But it hasn't yet, and the interim scrambling is called postmodernism.

✳

Books

Abrams, Jeremiah, ed. *Reclaiming the Inner Child*. Los Angeles: Jeremy P. Tarcher, 1990.

Academic American Encyclopedia. Danbury, Conn.: Grolier, 1993.

American Jurisprudence, 2d ed. Rochester, N.Y.: Lawyers Co-Operative Publishing Co., 1968.

American Pharmaceutical Association. *Handbook of Nonprescription Drugs*, 10th ed. Washington, D.C.: American Pharmaceutical Association.

Beranbaum, Rose Levy. *The Cake Bible*. New York: William Morrow and Co., 1988.

Black, Henry C., et al. *Black's Law Dictionary*. Saint Paul, Minn.: West Publishing Company, 1990.

Bray, Warwick, and David Trump. *The American Heritage Guide to Archaeology*. New York: American Heritage Press, 1970.

Chapman, Robert L., ed. *New Dictionary of American Slang*. New York: HarperCollins, 1986.

Claiborne, Robert. *Loose Cannons and Red Herrings*. New York: W. W. Norton & Co., 1988.

Cleckley, Hervey. *The Mask of Sanity*. New York: Plume, 1982.

Compton's Encyclopedia, Encyclopedia Britannica Educational Corporations, 1992.

Corsini, Raymond J., ed. *Encyclopedia of Psychology*, Vols. I, II, III. New York: John Wiley & Sons, 1994.

Covington, Philip A. *Computers: The Plain English Guide*. QNS Pub., 1991.

Coyle, L. Patrick. *The World Encyclopedia of Food*. New York: Facts on File, 1982.

Derfler, Fran, and Les Freed. *How Networks Work*. Emeryville, Calif.: Ziff-Davis, 1993.

Diagnostic and Statistical Manual of Mental Disorders, 3d ed. Washington, D.C.: American Psychiatric Press, 1980.

Dictionary of American History. New York: Charles Scribner's Sons, 1976.

Dowell, Philip, and Adrian Bailey. *Cook's Ingredients*. New York: Bantam Books, 1980.

Drexal, John, ed. *Facts on File Encyclopedia of the Twentieth Century*. New York: Facts on File, 1991.

Dugger, James A. *The New Professional*, 2d ed. Pacific Grove, Calif.: Brooks/Cole, 1975.

Edwards, Paul, ed. *Encyclopedia of Philosophy*, Vol I. New York: The Free Press, 1967.

Eidelburg, Ludwig, ed. *Encyclopedia of Psychoanalysis*. New York: The Free Press, 1968.

Encyclopedia Americana. Danbury, Conn.: Grolier, 1994.

Encyclopedia of World Art. New York: McGraw-Hill, 1959.

English, Horace B., and Ava Champney English. *A Comprehensive Dictionary of Psychological and Psychoanalytical Terms*. New York: David McKay Co., 1958.

Evans, Bergen. *A Dictionary of Contemporary American Usage*. New York: Galahad Books, 1981.

Facts on File Yearbook, 1987. New York: Facts on File, 1987.

Garner, Bryan A. *The Dictionary of Modern Legal Usage.* New York: Oxford University Press, 1987.

Gay, Peter. *Freud: A Life for Our Times.* New York: Norton, 1988.

Gifis, Steven H. *Law Dictionary.* Woodbury, N.Y.: Barron's, 1984.

Gillette, Peter A., and Paul Gillette. *Playboy's Book of Wine.* Playboy Press, 1974.

Glasse, Cyril. *Concise Encyclopedia of Islam.* San Francisco: HarperSanFrancisco, 1991.

Goldenson, Robert M. *Encyclopedia of Human Behavior,* Vol. I. New York: Doubleday, 1970.

Goldsborough, Reid. *Straight Talk About the Information Superhighway.* New York: Alpha Books, 1994.

Gregory, Richard L. *The Oxford Companion to the Mind.* New York: Oxford University Press, 1987.

Gurney, Gene, and Nick Apple. *The Library of Congress.* New York: Crown.

Hall, Calvin S. *A Primer of Freudian Psychology.* New York: New American Library, 1954.

Halsey, William D., ed. dir. *Collier's Encyclopedia.* New York: Macmillan, 1990.

Harre, Rom, and Roger Lamb, eds. *The Encyclopedic Dictionary of Psychology.* Cambridge, Mass.: MIT Press, 1983.

Hinnells, John R., ed. *Who's Who of World Religions.* New York: Simon & Schuster, 1992.

Hirsch, E. D., Jr., Joseph F. Kett, and James Trefil. *The Dictionary of Cultural Literacy.* Boston: Houghton Mifflin, 1988.

Holme, Richard, *Abnormal Psychology: Current Perspec-*

tives. Del Mar, Calif.: Communications Research Machines, Inc., 1972.

Houghton Mifflin staff, ed. *Wellness Encyclopedia*. Boston: Houghton Mifflin, 1992.

Laquey, Tracy. *Internet Companion*. Reading, Mass.: Addison-Wesley, 1994.

Islam and Islamic Groups: A Worldwide Reference Group. Detroit: Gale, 1992.

Janosik, Robert J., ed. *Encyclopedia of the American Judicial System*. New York: Macmillan, 1987.

Johnson, Thomas H. *Oxford Companion to American History*. New York: Oxford University Press, 1966.

Jung, C. G. *Four Archetypes*. Princeton: Princeton University Press, 1959.

Keesing's Record of World Events, 1988.

Larson, David E., ed. *Mayo Clinic Family Health Book*. New York: William Morrow, 1990.

Mackay, Charles. *Extraordinary Popular Delusions and the Madness of Crowds*. New York: Farrar, Straus and Giroux, 1932.

Macrae, R., R. K. Robinson, and M. J. Sadler, eds. *Encyclopaedia of Food Science, Food Technology, and Nutrition*. New York: Academic Press, 1993.

McGraw-Hill Encyclopedia of Science and Technology. New York: McGraw-Hill, 1987.

Menten, Theodore. *The Art Deco Style*. New York: Dover, 1972.

Microsoft Press staff, ed. *Microsoft Press Computer Dictionary*. Redmond, Wash.: Microsoft Press, 1993.

Montagné, Prosper. *New Larousse Gastronomique*. New York: Crown, 1977.

Morris, William, and Mary Morris. *Harper Dictionary of Contemporary Usage*. New York: HarperCollins, 1992.

————. *Dictionary of Words and Phrase Origins*. New York: HarperCollins, 1984.

Nagill, Frank N., ed. *World Philosophy*. Vol. 3: *1726–1896*. Los Angeles: Salem Press, 1982.

Nelton, Ian R. *Popular Dictionary of Islam*. Atlantic Highlands, N.J.: Humanities Press, 1992.

New American Encyclopedia. New York: Books, Inc., 1971.

New American Heritage Dictionary of the English Language.

O'Neill, Molly. *New York Cookbook*. New York: Workman Publishing, 1992.

Oran, Daniel, and Mark Tosti. *Law Dictionary for Non-Lawyers*. Saint Paul, Minn.: West Publishing, 1991.

Ortiz, Elisabeth Lambert. *The Encyclopedia of Herbs, Spices & Flavorings*. New York: Dorling Kindersley, 1992.

Partridge, Eric. *A Dictionary of Catch Phrases*, rev. ed. Lanham, MD: Madison Books, 1992.

Pearce, David W. *MIT Dictionary of Modern Economics*. Cambridge, Mass.: MIT Press, 1992.

Postman, Neil. *The Disappearance of Childhood*. New York: Dell, 1982.

Ramsey, Dan. *Weather Forecasting: A Young Meteorologist's Guide*. Blue Ridge Summit, Penn.: TAB Books, 1990.

Reese, W. L. *Dictionary of Philosophy and Religion*. Atlantic Highlands, N.J.: Humanities Press, 1980.

Reither, Joseph. *World History at a Glance*. New York: Barnes & Noble, 1952.

Ricklefs, Robert E. *The Economy of Nature*. New York: W. H. Freeman, 1993.

Rheingold, Howard, ed. *The Millennium Whole Earth Catalog*. San Francisco: HarperSanFrancisco, 1994.

Rieff, Philip. *Freud: The Mind of the Moralist*. New York: Doubleday, 1961.

Rogers, James. *The Dictionary of Clichés*. New York: Random House, 1992.

Rombauer, Irma S., and Marion Rombauer Becker. *Joy of Cooking*. New York: Bobbs-Merrill Co., 1975.

Rucker, Rudy, R. U. Sirius, and Queen Mu, eds. *Mondo 2000: A User's Guide to the New Edge*. New York: HarperPerennial, 1992.

Schmolling, Paul, William Burger, and Merrill Youkeles. *Helping People*. Englewood Cliffs, N.J.: Prentice-Hall, 1981.

Seltzer, Robert M. *Jewish People, Jewish Thought*. New York: Macmillan, 1982.

Shafritz, Jay M. *Dorsey Dictionary of American Government and Politics*. Chicago: Dorsey Press, 1988.

Shafritz, Jay M., et al. *Dictionary of Twentieth Century World Politics*. New York: Henry Holt & Co., 1993.

Shroyer, Jo A. *Quarks, Critters, and Chaos*. New York: Prentice-Hall, 1993.

Sills, David L., ed. *International Encyclopedia of the Social Sciences*, Vol 14. New York: Macmillan, 1968.

Stobart, Tom. *The Cook's Encyclopedia*. New York: Harper & Row, 1980.

Sutherland, Stewart. *International Dictionary of Psychology*. New York: Continuum Publishing Co., 1989.

Tannahill, Reay. *Food in History*. New York: Stein and Day, 1973.

Time-Life Books, *Complete Fix-It-Yourself Manual*. New York: Prentice Hall, 1989.

Tuchman, Barbara. *A Distant Mirror*. New York: Ballantine, 1978.

Tuleja, Thaddeus F. *Foreignisms*. New York: Macmillan, 1990.

Van Heuvelen, Alan. *Physics: A General Introduction*. Boston: Little, Brown and Co., 1982.

Vanoni, Marvin. *I've Got Goose Pimples*. New York: William Morrow, 1989.

Wall Street Guide to Understanding Money and Investment

Webber, Elizabeth, and Mike Feinsilber. *Grand Allusions*. Washington, D.C.: Farragut Publishing Co., 1990.

Weber, Eva. *Art Deco in America*. New York: Exeter Books, 1985.

West Publishing Company staff. *The Guide to American Law: Everybody's Legal Encyclopedia*. Saint Paul, Minn.: West Publishing Company, 1985.

White, Ron. *How Computers Work*. Emeryville, Calif.: Ziff-Davis, 1994.

Whitfield, Charles L. *Healing the Child Within*. Deerfield Beach, Fla.: Health Communications, Inc., 1987.

Whitehouse, Ruth D., ed. *The Facts on File Dictionary of Archaeology*. New York: Facts on File, 1983.

Wilson, Jerry D. *Physics: A Practical and Conceptual Approach*. Orlando, Fla.: Saunders College Publishing, 1989.

Wilson, Kenneth G. *Columbia Guide to Standard American English*. New York: Columbia University Press, 1993.

Wolfe, Tom. *From Bauhaus to Our House*. New York: Pocket Books, 1981.

Wolman, Benjamin B., ed. *Dictionary of Behavioral Science*. New York: Academic Press, 1989.

Zimmerman, David R. *Zimmerman's Complete Guide to Nonprescription Drugs*, 2d ed. Detroit: Gale, 1992.

Newspapers and Periodicals

Note: If an article is listed without an author the article had no byline.

Ajemian, Ronald G., and Albert B. Grundy. "Fiber Optics: The New Medium for Audio." *Journal of the Audio Engineering Society,* March 1990.

Allman, William F. "The Mathematics of Human Life." *U.S. News & World Report,* 14 June 1993.

Amato, Mary Koepke. "Kosher for Passover." *Washington Post,* 5 April 1993.

Anderson, Kurt. "Ted Goes Hollywood II." *Time,* 30 August 1993.

Anzelowitz, Lois. "Getting the Lead Out." *Working Woman,* September 1994.

"Area's Cellular Phone Industry Booms in 4 Years Since Its Birth." *Washington Post,* 30 November 1987.

Begley, Sharon. "The Endless Summer?" *Newsweek,* 11 July 1988.

Bennett, Ralph Kinney. "Pig Tales for Taxpayers." *Reader's Digest,* September 1991.

Berry, Jonathan. "What Is an Ad in the Interactive Future?" *Business Week,* 2 May 1994.

Brand, David. "Is the Earth Warming Up?" *Time,* 4 July 1988.

———. "Searching for Life's Elixir." *Time,* 12 December 1988.

Brody, Jane. "Personal Health: As saunas, hot tubs, and steam rooms multiply, so do disease-causing organisms." *New York Times,* 28 January 1987.

Brooke, James. "A New Coffee Cartel Tries Its Hand." *New York Times,* 3 October 1993.

Burkinshaw, Nic. "Going Behind Bars." *Electronics World + Wireless World*, February 1992.

Carlson, Peter. "The Spin Doctor Awards." *Washington Post Magazine*, 1 January 1989.

Carmeli, Yoram. "From Curiosity to Prop—A Note on the Changing Cultural Significances of Dwarves' Presentations in Britain." *Journal of Popular Culture*, Summer 1993.

Carpenter, Teresa. "Madonna's Doctor of Spin." *New York Times*, 13 September 1992.

Castro, Janice. "The Ultimate Mogul." *Time*, 19 April 1993.

"Cellular Phone Service Seen as Gold Mine." *Washington Post*, 21 November 1982.

Christian Science Monitor, "Power of Judicial Review, 11 February 1987."

Corliss, Richard. "Rock Goes Interactive." *Time*, 17 January 1994.

Deutschman, Alan. "Scramble on the Information Superhighway." *Fortune*, 7 February 1994.

Doan, R. Stephen. "Origins of Masonry." *Education* (Freemason publication), Fall 1993.

Elmer-Dewitt, Philip. "Battle for the Internet." *Time*, 25 July 1994.

"Fiberglass Is Possible Carcinogen." *New York Times*, 3 July 1994.

Franklin, Sarah. "Postmodern Mutant Cyborg Cinema." *New Scientist 22/29*, December 1990.

Gibbs, W. Wayt. "Practical Fractal." *Scientific American*, July 1993.

"A Glossary of Terms for Brews." *New York Times*, 11 July 1984.

Hall, Stephen S. "Garlic Power." *Health*, July/August 1994.

Huesner, Albert L. "Danger Zones." *American Baby*, October 1994.

Impoco, Jim. "America's Hippest Grandpa." *U.S. News & World Report,* 27 September 1993.

"Innovations: Calling Cars." *Washington Post,* 14 August 1984.

"The Internet." *PC Magazine,* 11 October 1994.

Jackson, James O. "Fascism Lives." *Time,* 6 June 1994.

Johnson, Rich. "Crystal Clear." *Trailer Life,* May 1989.

Klinkenborg, Verlyn. "Come boooossss!" [sic] *Smithsonian,* September 1993.

Kristof, Kathy M. "The Dow Jones Industrial Average." *Los Angeles Times,* 7 August 1994.

Lechner, Norbert. "A Disenchantment Called Postmodernism." *boundary 2,* a publication of Duke University Press, Fall 1993.

McAllister, Bill. "Pinning the Donkey, Elephant on the Parties." *Washington Post,* 3 November 1972.

Mead, Nathaniel. "Don't Drink Your Milk!" *Natural Health,* July/August 1994.

Murdoch, Guy. "A Consumer's Guide to Sun Protection." *Consumer's Research,* July 1994.

Nicholson, Paul J. "An Introduction to Fiber Optics." *Microwave Journal,* June 1991.

Norton, Erle, and Martin Du Bois. "Don't Call It a Cartel, but World Aluminum Has Forged a New Order." *Wall Street Journal,* 9 June 1994.

"Owens-Corning Introduces New Glass Fiber." *New York Times,* 23 September 1994.

Ponte, Lowell. "Why Our Hair Turns Gray." *Reader's Digest,* March 1991.

Press, Edward. "The Health Hazards of Saunas and Spas and How to Minimize Them." *American Journal of Public Health,* August 1991.

Prial, Frank J. "A Musty Myth." *New York Times Magazine,* 18 January 1987.

"Putting America On Line." *Washington Post*, 22 October 1989.

"Researchers Take a Step Toward a Technology Beyond Electronics." *Washington Post*, 21 December 1987.

"Romancing the Stone Age." *Utne Reader*, September/October 1993.

Safire, William. "Calling Dr. Spin." *New York Times Magazine*, 31 August 1986.

———. "Secs Appeal." *New York Times Magazine*, 26 January 1986.

———. "Tug of War." *New York Times Magazine*, 13 September 1987.

Samuelson, Robert J. "Lost on the Information Superhighway." *Newsweek*, 20 December 1993.

Schaefer, Bradley E. "The Green Flash." *Sky & Telescope*, February 1992.

"Secular Humanism: Meaning Varies with Political Stance." *New York Times*, 28 February 1986.

Shaffer, Richard A. "Consensus Computing." *Forbes*, 10 June 1991.

Stolberg, Sheryl. "The Little White Pill that Could." *Los Angeles Times*, 29 September 1994.

Taubes, Gary. "The Supercollider: How Big Science Lost Favor and Fell." *New York Times*, 26 October 1993.

Trépanier, Cécyle. "The Cajunization of French Louisiana: Forging a Regional Identity." *The Geographical Journal*, July 1991.

Tribe, Laurence H. "The Final Say." *New York Times Magazine*, 13 September 1987.

Uchitelle, Louis. "Job Extinction Evolving into a Fact of Life in U.S." *New York Times*, 24 March 1994.

Ullman, Dana. "Homeopathic Medicine: A Modern View." *Whole Earth*, Fall 1993.

Weiss, Gary. "Chaos Hits Wall Street—the Theory, That Is." *Business Week,* 2 November 1992.

Young, John Edward. "Mincemeat: A Tradition from the Middle Ages to Serve and Preserve." *Christian Science Monitor,* 7 November 1984.